VAGABOND CHRONICLES

Legacy or the Blue

Author, Capt. Eddie Gantner

VAGABOND CHRONICLES,

LEGACY OF THE BLUE.

Humorous anecdotes coupled with historic aviation events.

FIRST EDITION ISBN: 979-8-9917563-3-4

Library of Congress In Publication

Data Category: Biography, Aviation

Written by: Captain Eddie Gantner

Cover Design & Book Formatted by: Amazon Publishing

Printed in the United States by Amazon Publishing

10 9 8 7 6 5 4 3 2 1

Everyone Needs a Good 'Wingman.'

My Wingman's Call Sign's 'Lana!'

"One Must Wait Until the Evening to See How Splendid the Day Has Been."

— Sophocles

DEDICATION

This book is dedicated to professional pilots everywhere—not only major airline pilots but also those involved in every aviation endeavor that falls under that professional heading. They consist of flight instructors, commuter pilots, freight pilots, 'Non-Sked' pilots, and corporate/ charter pilots. Many of these pilots fly all types of aircraft, including very large and smaller ones, and all are held to the same standards of safety, sound judgment, and skill level as those applied to pilots who fly for major airlines. Several are employed by small, obscure companies whose pay scales are far less than those of the major airlines.

These dedicated professionals often lack union protection, which can hinder their ability to secure reasonable salaries and work conditions. Their duties are frequently more demanding than those of mainstream 'Legacy Pilots' and suffer from a lack of support systems that larger companies provide. Without the support of an advanced system, these pilots are on their own when confronted with unusual and challenging events that demand high skill and knowledge. Many in this group are overworked, underpaid, and underappreciated, but garner the respect of their peers as they provide needed services to the lay public while remaining invisible to many.

This book is further dedicated to the many 'cockpit colleagues' who have contributed their skill, knowledge, and scrutiny of my in-flight performance over the years. On many trips, under extreme circumstances requiring a heightened focus, alert thinking, and clear vision, they assisted in several successful airborne outcomes, often under dubious conditions. You know who you are. My hat is off to all of you.

Thank You!

ACKNOWLEDGMENT

So many wonderful folks, colleagues and non-colleagues alike, deserve credit for enticing me to write about my many memorable experiences. Over the years, I shared these experiences with many at parties and gatherings, usually relaying them while in a modified state of sobriety. Enthralled listeners (I like to think) said, "You need to put these stories in a book." Hearing that so often, I decided to give it a try. The first book was *Flying Vagabond*. I assign much of the credit for both books to my 'Wingman' Lana, for without her support, understanding, and love, neither that first book nor this would have happened. My late brother John was also an inspiration to me. He authored several books on his chosen profession, chiropractic. His encouragement and wisdom were greatly appreciated and are greatly missed.

I enjoyed many mentors along the way in my career. Still, I would be remiss if I didn't mention the late, great Captain Jimmy Ledbetter, whose mentoring, humor, skill, and utter disregard for convention inspired me to see beyond the curtain of the ordinary and to question the unquestionably accepted. His humor was often on display. On one memorable flight in a heavy four-engine transport aircraft (a British Argosy) that Jimmy was captaining, he graciously allowed me to fly from the left seat, the captain's seat, while he occupied my usual seat on the right. (A complete disregard for convention.)

The aircraft was on autopilot when Air Traffic Control told us to make an immediate left turn. Disengaging the autopilot, I ham-fistedly banked the aircraft briskly to the left, slightly exceeding thirty degrees. In doing so, I failed to maintain altitude, losing about two or three hundred feet. In bringing the aircraft back to the assigned altitude, I put a couple of 'G's' on the plane. Jimmy, looking up from his *Playboy* magazine and in his inimical south Detroit accent, said: "Jesus Gantner, I can't even turn the freakin page," referring, of course, to the heavy 'G' load I put on the aircraft.

Perhaps not funny now, but amusing and embarrassing then. Captain Jimmy was the only one of many captains I flew with who allowed me to swap seats. For many years, I have kept his gracious generosity, easy smile, and mantle of warm friendship in fond remembrance. Another hilarious Jimmy story awaits the reader in Chapter One.

CONTENTS

FOREWORD

It is a distinct pleasure to introduce the reader to Captain Eddie Gantner. He is the author of *Flying Vagabond*; his sequel continues his exciting exploits through the capricious ocean far above the Earth. Captain Eddie Gantner, author, orator, confidant, actor, Quiet Birdman, and professional airline transport pilot, is also one of the very few pilots to have been honored by the Federal Aviation Administration (FAA) for his fifty-plus years' service to the enhancement and safety of commercial aviation.

I met Captain Eddie in September 2008. CAE (Canadian Aviation Electronics) Flight Training Center hired experienced airline transport-rated pilots to train corporate pilots flying the Hawker Beechcraft 700, 800, and 1000 series twin-jet aircraft. Most companies operating these aircraft were charter companies under FAA Part 135 regulations. (Airlines operated under FAA Part 121 regulations, each equally stringent.) Pilots were required to complete training every six months, with a qualifying check ride conducted annually to assess and certify their piloting proficiency.

Together, Eddie, my colleagues, and I embarked on a mission to ensure each pilot's proficiency in operating within the standards demanded by the FAA. Our collective efforts led Captain Eddie and me to the esteemed 'Lead Flight Instructor' position at CAE.

This was a significant milestone in our journey, as CAE was renowned for building flight simulators for military and civilian air carrier operations.

Capt. Eddie is the most personable person I know and is my good friend. Our frequent get-togethers inevitably devolve into discussions of a particular aviation accident and what might have been done differently to protect the crew and innocent passengers. Eddie felt the main problems were pilot overload and an overreliance on cockpit automation—pilots relying too heavily on in-flight computers. Piloting high-performance jet aircraft sans computers is a highly perishable skill that must be continually practiced. These skills are called 'Raw Data Skills.' Eddie developed a PowerPoint presentation identifying and integrating these issues into ground school curricula. The program opened creative discussions on how to fall back from an overreliance on automation to basic piloting skills. Eddie and I felt a better understanding of aircraft performance was sorely needed. We instituted a more user-friendly approach to this most important, often misunderstood subject.

Flying is safe! Aircraft, by design, result from calculus designed into the metal and carbon fiber. It is, after all, a machine and is subject to occasional minor failures with the potential to morph into more serious situations. It is up to the pilot to understand and react appropriately during these times of high-stress warnings.

On occasion, while flying, both Eddie and I had to deal with problems that required immediate and proper action and reaction to solve unexpected issues.

Not only are the pages illustrative of Eddie's adventures, but the reader will also be treated to an exciting recap of some of aviation's heroes, events, and history. As you turn the pages of these exciting, often humorous, and always adventurous (and sometimes historic) escapades, sit back, relax, and enjoy a glass of wine as you ride along.

Respectfully,

Captain William Leonard, Boeing 757/767

United Airlines (Ret

PREFACE

As we progress through childhood, adolescence, and adulthood, it one day occurs to us that we can no longer rely on family members or anyone else to sustain our life's journey. Often, when that realization sets in, one may be filled with anxiety, trepidation, and fear. For many of us, those feelings ignite a self-discovery that leads to a 'river' whose swift current offers great promise to those who dare to get wet. Sadly, many never reach this river. The river could be called fate, destiny, or just plain luck.

I often wonder how one becomes an expert at a particular skill or trade that held no fascination in earlier years. How did Eddie Rickenbacker, a famous WWI flying ace, develop an interest in flying when he had absolutely zero interest from an early age, terrified of heights and suffering from vertigo at the thought of them? How did he become the most famous American flying ace of WWI? He was awarded the Medal of Honor on November 6, 1930, which replaced his Distinguished Service Cross awarded in 1918. In 1938, hearing that General Motors was selling Eastern Air Transport, he purchased the airline for 3.5 million, becoming the president and chairman of the board of Eastern Airlines. By his admission, "I have led a charmed life," which would manifest once again in surviving 21 days in an open raft, drifting for hundreds of miles in the Pacific after the ocean ditching of the B-17 he was a passenger in.

This was the third aircraft crash he had survived; charmed indeed!

And what about General Jimmie Doolittle, who went from a wooden frame house on a tundra in Nome, Alaska, to becoming a prize-fighter with no interest in what was later called aviation until ultimately earning a degree in aeronautical science and engineering from MIT, pioneering the development of 'blind' flying instrumentation, allowing pilots to fly into clouds solely relying on those flight instruments, proving it was indeed possible. Modern aircraft routinely take off and land in any weather using nothing but their aircraft instruments, thanks to the 'spark' that ignited Doolittle's passion. He eventually led the famous WWII 'Doolittle Raid,' launching B-25 Bombers from the deck of an aircraft carrier in the mid-Pacific to bomb Tokyo. Never before had twin-engine bombers been launched from an aircraft carrier. Aviation owes an outstanding debt to Jimmy Doolittle, a physically short man but a giant in aviation.

General Doolittle was awarded the Medal of Honor in April 1942.

Every schoolboy in the mid-20th century recognized the name 'Charles Lindbergh.' Charles was raised on a farm in rural Minnesota and had never seen an airplane. In 1912, at age ten, Charles's mother, Evangeline, took him to an airshow in Virginia during a trip to Washington, DC. Aircraft were a rare sight in the early part of the 20th century. Charles later wrote, "I knew then that I would one day fly." The 'spark,' once ignited, burned brightly.

Orville Wright's prognostication of "No flying machine will ever fly from New York to Paris" was based on his belief that all airplanes would be as slow as his Wright Flyer. Lindbergh shattered Wright's opinion using a more advanced aircraft engine when he took the Spirit of St. Louis down a muddy runway on Roosevelt Field, Long Island, one rainy morning in May 1927 and landed at Paris' Le Bourget Field 28 hours later.

A Special Act of Congress awarded Lindbergh the Medal of Honor on December 14, 1927, although it was almost always awarded for heroism in combat. President Coolidge presented it to Lindbergh at the White House on March 21, 1928.

Years later, while working with Dr. Alexis Carrel, the Nobel Prize-winning French surgeon Charles invented the glass perfusion pump, making it possible for organs to remain viable outside of the body during surgical procedures, making future heart surgeries possible, and eventually leading to the construction of the first heart-lung machine. That innovation is still considered to be a significant advancement in the fields of open-heart surgery and organ transplantation. Lindbergh played a substantial role in the development of the device. In recognition of their groundbreaking work, Carrel (years earlier awarded the Nobel Prize for developing a vascular suturing technique still in use today) and Lindbergh appeared on the cover of *Time* magazine on June 13, 1938.

These scientific and aviation breakthroughs came from men who would become legends and are revered for their vision and exploits today. These were 'committed' people who dared to step into the swift current of the 'river,' setting them on that path of self-discovery and igniting that hidden 'spark' of passion along their life journey.

Admittedly, it took me a while to find this 'river,' but I took the plunge once I did. I discovered a love of aviation and flying, leading to a beautiful, fulfilling life of adventures and thrills, visited many places I would never have otherwise and chronicled adventures I never dreamed of in my earlier book, *Flying Vagabond*.

Further tales of the *Vagabond*, both personal and historical, are revealed and reviewed as the journal is once again opened to adventure and adrenaline!

Lindbergh, Dr. Carrel and the perfusion pump

Fasten Your Seat Belt!

Captain Eddie!

Prologue
"THE COORS CAPER"

Has anyone heard of Coors bootlegging besides *Smokey and the Bandit*? The true Coors bootlegging story dates back to the early 20th century when Adolf Coors, founder of the Coors Brewing Company, began brewing beer in the Rocky Mountains of Colorado. In the early 20th century, Coors beer was popular in the west but was not sold east of the Mississippi River. This caused a massive demand for the beer, leading opportunistic entrepreneurs to transport the beer across the country illegally, thus creating the first-ever major 'bootlegging' operations.

The practice of bootlegging Coors beer became so popular that it was even featured in movies such as the above-mentioned *Smokey and the Bandit* and many TV shows as a way of life for the adventurous and daring. While it is no longer illegal to transport the beer across the country, the true Coors bootlegging story lives on in the pages of history. Here is a bit of lesser-known history that, until now, I don't believe has been mentioned on any pages.

My introduction to what I now call 'The Coors Caper' took place in the late 1960s as a pilot flying automotive parts to several cities west of the Mississippi. I had never tasted Coors before being offered one with dinner while on a RON (Rest Over Night) in Kansas City, MO. I was not a beer drinker per se, but I liked that can of Coors. It tasted even better when I discovered it could not be purchased east of the Mississippi River due to outdated interstate laws and several other reasons, not the least of which was that the large eastern breweries recognized Coors as a high-end beer and feared the competition. Their combined political power succeeded in halting further eastern distribution.

I was a co-pilot on a DC-6/7 aircraft flying with a captain I will refer to as Capt. Ben. I had never flown with Capt. Ben before. He was a soft-spoken, fun-loving professional who was also, I discovered, a bootlegger. Oh, not like Al Capone or any real-life gangsters; nope. Capt. Ben just made the rounds of several liquor stores while in Coors Country, buying up 10 or 20 cases of Coors at a time for later sale or distribution to a few of his eastern friends. Coors sold for about $3.50 to $4.00 a case then, as I recall. Ben would sell it for $6.00 a case on our return to Detroit.

Captain Ben's enterprise quickly developed into a legend among flight crews, sparking entrepreneurial endeavors among several thirsty airmen. Soon, 'Coors Cargo' became the cargo load du jour while infrequently 'deadheading' back to home base with aircraft semi-loaded with Coors. The realization that this was many times more illegal than fun hardly ever dawned on anyone until, inevitably, someone blew the whistle on Ben's enterprise. He and his crew were caught with 5 cases of Coors on his DC-6 while landing at YIP (Detroit's Willow Run airport) from Kansas City. (A light load for him). This would be the last time he transported 'The Nectar of the Gods' across state lines. Someone had tipped off the ATF (Alcohol, Tobacco, and Firearms).

Several armed agents had been waiting for Ben to land. Fortunately, he didn't have his usual ten or twenty cases on board, convincing the agents that those five were for his and his crew's consumption. According to the agents, it was still wrong and illegal, but it was understandable, as they also liked the stuff.

Ben and his crew were taken into custody and later released. A fine of a couple of thousand dollars each, a pilot license suspended, and a threat of prison time under the RICO Act prompted the immediate hiring of counsel. RICO charges were eventually dropped against Ben and the crew. It was later determined that the co-pilot and flight engineer were unwilling partners in crime, and all pending charges and fines were rescinded. Their FAA licenses were eventually reinstated; however, the airline refused to rehire them. Capt. Ben, being only a couple of months away from mandatory retirement of 60 years, never returned to flying.

(Today, under FAR 121, you may fly until age 65 and, perhaps soon, 67 due to the current pilot shortage.)

Not long after my innocent introduction to bootlegging on an industrial scale as Capt. As Ben's co-pilot, I was upgraded to captain status as a C-46 captain. On one of my first trips to MKC (Kansas City, MO), remembering Capt. Ben's enterprise before he was busted, I also indulged in the nefarious transporting of what became known as 'The Nectar of the Gods.' Unlike Capt. Ben, however, this wasn't a money-making enterprise for me but rather a fun way to enjoy a great beer and snub our noses at what we considered unfair to appreciative beer drinkers everywhere.

As luck would have it, on my very first deadheading return trip to YIP from MKC (Kansas City, MO) with 3 cases of Coors on board, another of our company aircraft heard me on the ATC freq. and asked me to come up on a discrete, somewhat secure frequency not used by ATC at the time.

Acknowledging and switching frequencies, I heard: "Hey, Eddie, are you up?" (On freq..) "Yup. What's going on?"

"Are you carrying cargo?" "No, deadheading; (Empty) why?"

"You carrying anything else?" (Coors on board?) "Yup! A few."

"Rumor has it the ATF has gotten wind of pilots flying brew back to Detroit and is beginning to check all inbound freighter aircraft landing at YIP sporadically. Don't land at YIP; divert to DTW.

The weather is crap at YIP anyway. Just claim it was below minimums with better weather at DTW. Billie Dale, the ramp guy at Butler Aviation, is a friend of mine and has a pickup truck that will take it off your hands. Just tell him you're a friend of mine. I don't think the ATF is there. Good luck!"

After contacting ATC with a change of destination, we were radar vectored to DTW for landing. The weather at DTW was right at landing minimums. After securing the aircraft, Billie was located, Coors was offloaded, and the day was saved—so was the beer. Whew!

Later, when many of the crews heard Capt. Ben got busted, this nefarious undertaking was immediately halted. This had been the first and last time I transported 'The Nectar of the Gods.'

I never really considered it a crime at the time; instead, it was just a fun thing to do. Of course, Ben was selling the stuff, exponentially increasing his threat potential.

A few of us who had engaged in something approaching the industrial smuggling employed by Capt. Ben, later that evening, hosted a FINALE party among a trusted and select group of friends at the Knob Hill Apartments, where most of us lived very near Willow Run Airport. Toasting our good fortune of avoiding the Feds and savoring the last of the Golden Brew, we collectively agreed the risk to career and life was not worth the potential upheaval when we could still drink it west of the Mississippi!

Coors beer was first sold nationally in 1978 and was available in every state. However, until then, it was only legal to sell in 11 states. Those states included Colorado, Oregon, Washington, Idaho, Wyoming, Montana, California, Utah, South Dakota, North Dakota, and New Mexico. I suspect some clandestine flights were made to the Motor City then. By 1984, it was in 36 states. Today, it is in all 50 states.

Golden memories of a golden brew from Golden, Colorado, were made more delicious because it was as forbidden as the apple. Those good 'ole golden days still bring me a good 'ole golden smile!

Chapter One
"HOW DO YOU LIKE THEM APPLES?"

S t. Louis was cold in January. The snow had recently stopped, covering the dreaded black ice perfectly. We barely had eight hours of rest when dispatch called, alerting us to the 0700 proposed departure. After a quick shave and shower, we were off to the airport.

Arriving just as our freight had been loaded, a flight plan was filed for Cleveland while the aircraft was being de-iced. I was flying the right seat and was a reasonably new first officer with the airline. My captain was Jim Ledbetter, whose accent had you believing he was from way down Dixie Way. He was from South Detroit.

When I asked him about his accent, he mentioned that his dad was from Mississippi, and he had a severe Dixie accent. "Guess I just picked it up from him and never lost it."

We were flying a Curtiss-Wright C-46 for Zantop Air Transport based in Detroit, MI. Loading was completed, the aircraft was de-iced, and we started the engines. Taxi clearance was received for Runway 12L. The plane was loaded to maximum gross weight. Taxing over a few of the splotches of black ice, the aircraft had a slight tendency to skid and slip. Capt. Jim had more than a few hours in command of a C-46 and handled it well. We reached the aircraft's 'run-up pad' and commenced our preflight engine checks as Capt. Jim began the mandatory Mag check (Magnetos). The left Mag had an unacceptable drop for flight. The 'burnout' procedure often 'cured' that problem, but required a couple of minutes to complete.

We were number one for takeoff and advised the tower we required about two minutes before we could go.. It was rush hour in St Louis. TWA, whose home base was, and Ozark Airlines, whose hub was also STL, began to stack up behind us. Directly behind us were a few Boeing's whose wingspan precluded them from getting around us. As Jim ran up the left engine per procedure, I noticed an Ozark Airlines DC-9-10 (the smallest of the DC-9 family) snaking around the Boeing's as his wingspan was much shorter. As he passed us, he called the tower. "Ozark 659 number one, ready for take off."

"Zantop 613Z, I thought you were number one for take off," responded the tower.

"We were!" Jim responded, "Until this 'dipstick pulled in front of us. You almost clipped us with your tail, Ozark!"

Ozark 659, keying his mike, replied: "How do you like them apples?"

"Ozark 659, Tower; Are you clear of the aircraft in the run-up pad?"

"Affirmative, Ozark 659."

The tower had no choice but to clear Ozark for takeoff. "Fly runway heading, Contact Departure on 124.7."

Now Capt. Jim was just a little more than pissed off, calling them sobs and everything else one can imagine. As Ozark commenced its takeoff roll, Jim had an inspiration. Behind his seat and attached to the bulkhead was a huge fire bell that would trigger an alert of an engine fire. The fire warning in C-46 aircraft necessitated a large bell to be heard over the roar of the two PW-R2800 engines during flight. Grabbing his microphone, Capt. Jim placed it next to the bell while simultaneously pressing the transmit button on the mic and the 'fire bell' test button; he gazed down the runway. Instantly, the Ozark DC-9 commenced a high-speed aborted takeoff as speed brakes and thrust reversers were deployed. The aircraft fishtailed a bit as it slowed.

"Ozarks aborting."

"Ozark, do you have a problem?" asked the tower.

"Yeah, we heard a fire bell.

Tower responded: "So did we!"

TWA 811 transmitted, "TWA 811 heard it!"

"TWA 412 heard it also,"...and on and on.

Jim patiently waited for an opportunity to break into the transmission, "How Do You Like Them Apples? Zantop 613Z, Number One, Ready for Take off."

You could almost hear the applause from the other aircraft behind us.

Chapter Two
"STEPS FROM DISASTER"

Note the Ladder

The ceiling was reportedly at landing minimums of 200' and ½ mile. The weather was absolute crap as we arrived at Kansas City. (Furloughed from Zantop, I was now flying as captain for Shamrock Airlines.) We set up the instrument approach to Rwy19 at MKC. With the landing gear and flaps extended, I flew the aircraft to the minimum approach altitude.

"Minimums! Runway not in sight!" yelled my first officer.

I immediately commenced a missed approach.

Kansas City Downtown Airport lies almost at the city's base, whose buildings protrude ominously above the airport elevation (700' and change). With towers to the left of the runway center-line as well as a 1500' MSL obstacle (more towers) along the center-line of the runway about 4 miles out, it is a freaking place to put an airport.

The missed approach procedure called for an immediate climbing left turn to 4,000' and then a holding fix. Switching to departure control frequency, we asked for another go. I wanted to proceed to our alternate airport, St. Louis, but we had cargo for MKC, not STL, so we tried again.

Receiving radar vectors, we again intercepted the final approach course for the ILS (Instrument Landing System) approach to Rwy19.

"Minimums, runway in sight, take over visually," yelled my F/O

"Whew, that was fun," I said. "Call ops and tell them we are taxiing in case they weren't on tower freq."

My professional aviation career started when I was hired to co-pilot a C-46 for Zantop Air Transport, later Universal Airlines. The company ceased operations in 1971 when Shamrock Airlines hired me as a C-46 captain. Shamrock Airlines was a newcomer to the automotive cargo-hauling business based at YIP (Willow Run Airport, Ypsilanti, MI). I was, once again, flying the venerable C-46. Their fleet consisted of 3 C-46 and 2 DC-6 aircraft.

They had only recently been granted an FAA Part 121 Supplemental Certificate and wasted no time applying it to operations. It was not precisely a shoestring operation; they lacked the sophistication and coordination I was used to. However, a job was a job, and I wasn't complaining. (At least not loudly.)

The cargo ramp was the same I had been on so many times with Zantop and Universal. Many of the ramp personnel were also the same. When realizing I was now flying 'Dumbo' for Shamrock, I was greeted like a long-lost cousin. Smiles and handshakes were the order of the day—or night, as it was just beyond midnight.

Entering operations, I was informed that instead of returning directly to Willow Run, we would make an unscheduled stop at St. Louis. I wanted to get home as this was Christmas Eve.

Our unloading and departure for STL were accomplished in record time, as everyone wanted to get home. We were only on the ground in STL for about thirty minutes as some minor company material was put aboard. *Couldn't they mail it? Damn!*

Take off and climb out from St. Louis were somewhat normal. The '46' climb speed was usually 125 knots. During the climb to 5,000 ft, I noticed a slight pulsing of the elevator controls. *Hmm! It's not severe, but it shouldn't be there.* My FO was oblivious, so I said nothing, but the concern was mounting.

As the aircraft reached five thousand feet, climb power was reduced to a cruise power setting. When the plane accelerated, the pulsing became more noticeable, pronounced, and concerning. *Geez! Now What?*

Reducing power, I asked my co-pilot to grab onto the controls and tell me what he felt. He almost immediately confirmed the pulsing I had felt. Indianapolis was at our twelve o'clock position and some 50 miles distant. I immediately requested a diversion to Indy. I didn't know what was happening, but I did know we needed to land right freakin' now!

As the aircraft slowed, the elevator control column oscillated less. The landing was normal, but curiosity was off the peg. Upon landing, the co-pilot was to proceed aft, open the cargo door, and place the access ladder, hooking and locking it firmly in place for egress. He was also tasked with pulling it and putting it on board for departure.

On landing in Indy, I quickly secured the engine. Leaping from my seat, I pushed him out of the way, going aft to the door. Anxiety had got the better of me as I pushed the cargo door open. My first officer standing directly behind me said: "Oh Shit!"

Given the circumstances, this was, at the very least, an understatement. Staring up at us was—wait for it...the ladder that had never been brought aboard. The procedure was for the co-pilot to haul the 50-lb. metal ladder in before closing the cargo loading door. It was readily apparent that in his haste, he got out of sequence and failed to bring the ladder aboard, thus disrupting airflow over the elevator controls.

Since we were departing STL early in the morning, no other aircraft were behind us to warn us of an impending in-flight problem. The adage 'haste makes waste' was applied in spades.

The ladder was metallic and heavy. Two snap locks on the top of each ladder post secured it to the aircraft. Only one was still attached and locked. I can only imagine what damage a 50+ lb. ladder, descending at terminal velocity, would do to an automobile or roof. Shaken and stirred, I could only manage a "Dude, WTF?" Enough said! Our call sign that night should have been 'Angel Flight One.'

Chapter Three
"DARK SKY, LIGHT TOUCH"

"Dumbo" C-46

Since the invention of powered flight, engine failures have been reported, whether from piston, turboprop, or jet engines. They are always unexpected, always problematic, and frequently an emergency. It is said, "A pilot flies an aircraft with his head, not his hands." While true, it helps to have a great pair of hands to assist in the mental formulation of options during the dire moments between engine failure recognition and immediate action.

As one of two newly hired C-46 captains, I was told I would be temporarily assigned to a base in San Juan, Puerto Rico, pending requested approval from the Puerto Rican airport authorities. Until then, I was assigned to general cargo-hauling duties, hauling mostly automobile parts for the Big Three Automakers, as they were known at the time, from Detroit's Willow Run

Airport. The airline was understaffed, so all crews were kept exceptionally busy. It was not unusual for us to barely become legal to fly after our mandatory eight hours of rest when we were back in the air. I was rapidly becoming more recurrent in the aircraft daily.

And so it was, on a particularly dark and stormy night, that I was dispatched with a split cargo load for the GM plant in Linden, N.J., followed by a general cargo load to be delivered to Sanford, Maine.

General Motors has a massive plant in Linden. The factory was immediately adjacent and almost co-located on the Linden airport property. At the time, there was no instrument approach to the runway.

The weather deteriorated rapidly as we approached the East Coast. The only option available was an approach to the Teterboro Airport, N.J. Approaching TEB, we were issued a 'hold for traffic' as the airspace was saturated with IFR traffic; the weather had caused delays at all three New York and New Jersey airports. The hold lasted for 30 minutes. Cleared to depart the holding fix, we were radar vectored for an ILS approach to Rwy19 at TEB, where the weather was reported to be at landing minimums for the approach: 300' and 3/4 mi. A gusty 30 to 40-degree crosswind of 15 to 20 knots made for a turbulent instrument approach. Adding to the challenge, the ceiling was reported as a ragged 300 ft. A near-missed approach was averted when the runway suddenly and barely appeared through the rain. The C-46 was a difficult aircraft to land in normal circumstances; the downpour, accompanied by a nasty crosswind, provided an added challenge.

Upon arriving at the Atlantic Aviation ramp, GM, knowing full well that a landing at Linden was not an option that evening, dispatched an 18-wheeler to Atlantic TEB to collect their cargo. Two heavy pallets of auto parts were offloaded while we refueled for our next stop in Sanford, Maine. We still had three pallets aboard, with a combined weight of 4,000 pounds. Eight hundred gallons of 100LL fuel were uploaded, approximately 5,000 pounds, which brings our takeoff weight to 40,000 pounds (max takeoff weight, 48,000 pounds).

A temporary ground stop was in effect for weather in the area, causing lengthy delays. Departing and landing aircraft were stacked up and backed up in the air and on the ground. Ground control asked if we could accept Rwy24 for takeoff. It was shorter by 1,000'. The wet runways and the extra thousand feet on Rwy19 played a large part in most jet aircraft's acceleration/stop distance. Although a consideration, our old C-46 had no such restrictions. We readily accepted. The wind was out of the west at 15 to 20 with gusts now to 30 knots.

"How much time would you require before you could accept a takeoff clearance when advised?" asked the ground controller.

"If we could position now to the departure end of Runway 24 and perform our engine run-ups, we could accept an immediate takeoff clearance," I responded.

"Roger. You are cleared to start engines. Report ready to taxi."

Engines were started, and taxi clearance was received. A hurried engine run-up and mag check at the Rwy24 hold short line put us at number one for takeoff. Ten minutes later, the ground stop was lifted, and a takeoff clearance was issued, including instructions to climb to and maintain 1500 ft, then an immediate right turn to a heading of 270 to keep us clear of the significant New York airspace.

The weather had not changed much from our earlier approach

and landing. Cockpit procedures immediately after takeoff in 'Ole Dumbo' (C-46 nickname) were primarily accomplished with hand signals, as any attempt at speech would be drowned out by the high-decibel rumblings of both Pratt & Whitney R-2800s.

A thumbs-up signal to the first officer translated to 'gear-up,' while a one index finger signal translated to 'First Power Reduction to METO' (Max Except Takeoff) power. Conversely, a two-finger signal translates to 'Reduce Power to Climb Power.'

The takeoff was normal until the signal was given for power to be reduced to METO. As throttles were gently pulled back from the takeoff setting of 52 inches of manifold pressure by the FO, a sudden lurch of the aircraft to the right and a simultaneous momentary flare of color against the three-hundred-foot overcast was accompanied by a relatively significant reduction of right engine manifold pressure to something south of 30 inches of manifold pressure. (Normal takeoff manifold pressure is 52 inches.) Some right engine malfunctions coupled with a wa-wa sound indicated out-of-sync engines. Immediately leveling the aircraft to stay below the 300' overcast and taking stock of its flyability, I increased the right engine throttle to recapture some power, but to no avail.

"Feather #2 engine!" I yelled.

As I increased to takeoff power on the #1 engine, I yelled, "Declare an emergency."

"Shamrock 902F is declaring an emergency!" The FO changed the transponder to Squawk 7700.

The tower controller responded quickly in a somewhat stunned tone: "Shamrock, say again?"

"Shamrock 902F is declaring an emergency, Squawking 7700!" the FO responded in a voice bordering panic.

(Of course, flying the airplane is more important than radioing your plight to a person on the ground incapable of understanding it, but it sure is a clever idea at times).

The tower controller asked, "What are your intentions, Shamrock?"

"Tell 'em we have one feathered and attempting to stay visual with the airport for a low close-in visual approach back to Runway 1 at TEB," I yelled!

"Fuel and souls aboard?" he responded.

"Tell him what he wants to know," I yelled.

It should be stated here that the C-46 we were flying was incredibly old and not equipped with boom mikes, with only old WWII headsets. It was antiquated. Consequently, all communication was done with a handheld mike, which made it cumbersome at best during an emergency and not great during regular times. I was too busy attempting to keep the bloody aircraft in the air, relying on my FO for all communication. (The company soon rectified the headset issue after my briefing back at home base.)

The stress in the tower controller's voice was apparent as he announced the airport was closed due to an emergency in progress to Runway 1 at TEB. I am sure the New York TRACON controller's blood pressure shot off the charts as the already saturated airspace became a literal 'Warren of Metal' in the murky gray skies of New York.

I knew many tower obstructions from many past visits to TEB. My obvious concern was staying close to the airport during the return circle, as the wind was almost due west. I did not want to overshoot the final approach to Rwy1. This would be somewhat of a downwind landing, but that couldn't be helped.

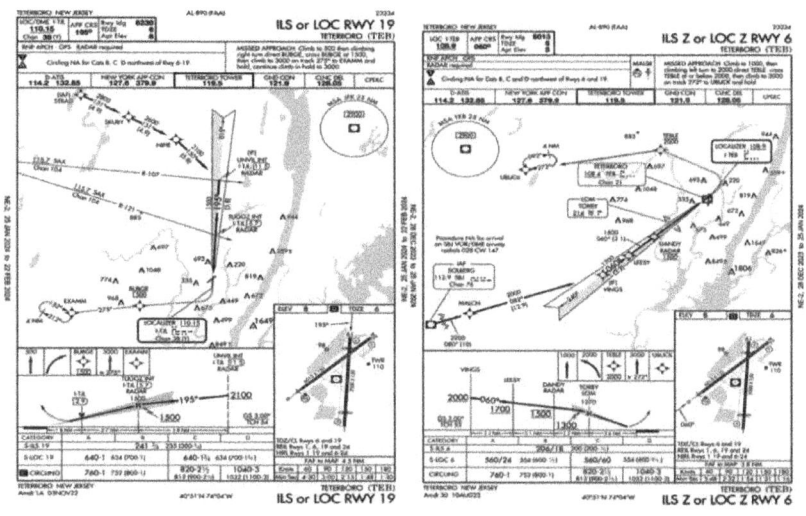

The above charts show several obstructions south of Runway 19 and the approach end of Runway 6, the reciprocal of the runway we had just departed.

Speed was a concern; however, I discovered I could maintain a reasonably steady 100 knots in buffeting turbulence. The rain was heavy at times, but thankfully, the large side DV (direct vision) windows provided a clearer view of the airport environment, looking left as I banked the aircraft onto a base leg.

The rain pelted the windscreen with a vengeance, leaking into the cockpit to form a pool of cold water in my lap. (The C-46 was not a pressurized aircraft and usually leaked when flying through rain.

It also leaked on approach, but I had a poncho on my lap to catch the water. It was a part of a C-46 pilot's retinue of required equipment. Sadly, I had failed to put it on my lap for takeoff.)

There was little time for checklists as I called and signaled, "Gear Down!" Glancing at the left engine cylinder head temp, I saw that it was approaching the red arc as I maintained a high-power setting. The buffeting crosswind became more problematic as we approached the runway. Speed maintenance, especially since we were landing downwind, was an issue. Fearful of the tower obstructions I could not see but knew were there, I found I was too close to the runway. "Full Flaps Now!" I yelled in my best adrenaline-soaked voice. Rolling out on a quarter-mile final and slightly high, we were pelted with a gusty and buffeting wind of over 30 knots. There were no windscreen wipers to help mitigate the rain, which caused the runway lights to 'star,' scattering and diffusing the light, making a problematic visual landing approach much more difficult.

The last speed I remember was just south of 80 knots when crossing the runway end, bouncing slightly on touchdown. Thank God for the very large ailerons on the C-46. I could keep it straight with immediate and reasonable control inputs, but stopping was another matter. There was no anti-skid on Dumbo as the wheels began to hydroplane.

The wheel brakes were ineffective during those moments as the wheels stopped turning because of the hydroplaning. Fortunately, with such a large amount of drag, we quickly slowed, and braking, once again, became effective. Finally, we could clear the runway and switch to ground control frequency, and we were cleared to taxi to Atlantic Aviation.

Ground advised us to expect an FAA inspector to greet us at Atlantic. They (the FAA) had been monitoring the tower frequency and called for a briefing. The arriving Fed was a retired Navy man. He requested a written report, which I happily supplied. Climbing aboard the aircraft and noticing the wet seats, "You guys didn't piss yourselves, did ya?" he asked tongue in cheek—a comedian in a Fed disguise.

We later found that we had blown a jug due to a split intake manifold. My attempt at increasing power on the right engine exacerbated the situation, leaving us no choice but to feather the engine to reduce drag.

There are many cute aviation sayings that you may come across over time. One thing that comes to mind when reliving this event is that "You get experience only after you need it!" This was undoubtedly one of those situations. I was not sure I would be ready for another blown jug anytime soon, but at least now, I have had the required experience.

Chapter Four
"THE SHEPHERD'S HOOK"

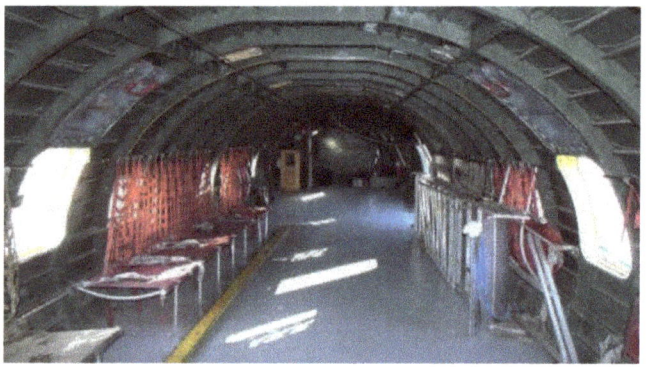

The "Shepherd's Hook" is the red line across the aft bulkhead!

Only a few C-46s survive; some are still hauling cargo in Alaska, and others are doing the same south of the border. Curtis had originally built the C-46 Commando, hoping to sell it to the airlines of the day. A takeoff accident occurred on its first demo flight in front of many hopeful airline dignitaries, sealing its fate as an airline passenger carrier.

The cause of the accident was quickly and easily determined; the control locks had not been removed from the horizontal stabilizer. Although it was the first accident involving the control locks on this model, time proved it was not the last.

The military, however, recognized its unique capability and established a remarkable reputation during WWII. The aircraft quickly earned the nickname 'The Whale' and sometimes 'The Curtis Calamity.' The US Navy/ Marine Corps also operated and renamed them the R5C. A more recent nickname is 'Dumbo.'

With three times the cargo and passenger carrying capacity of its nearest competitor, the DC-3, its two Pratt & Whitney R-2800 turbocharged engines allowed it to climb above the dizzying heights of many Himalayan peaks between India and China. When 717 miles of the Burma Road between the two countries was captured and closed by the Japanese Empire in 1942, it was the only way to keep the flow of supplies moving to China. Fatally dangerous and woefully inadequate at times, it nonetheless saved many lives by supplying much-needed military and humanitarian aid to a now isolated and desperate China.

A unique characteristic of the C-46 was its retractable tail wheel. It is the only 'tail dragger' of its kind with this feature. A means was provided to lower the tail wheel manually for landing, should it become necessary. This was accomplished by a long hook called 'The shepherd's hook.'

It can be seen on the aft cabin bulkhead, depicted by the red line stretching left to right horizontally in the picture. Not seen is a small opening through the aft bulkhead through which the long hook could be extended, snagging the over-center strut of the tail wheel and pulling it. Hopefully, the tail wheel would extend and, with the assistance of an air load, would lock into place. Access to this hook was mandatory and necessary.

I had been TDY (Temporary duty) to San Juan, Puerto Rico, supplying all types of cargo to the Caribbean Islands. Often, the aircraft would be bulked out with oversized boxes and equipment.

The very aft bay in the plane was called the 'J' compartment. While freight could be loaded in that section, it was done to provide easy access to that shepherd's hook.

Our Puerto Rican freight loader was Manuel, a dynamic, pleasant young man. Despite my constant explanation of the necessity of reaching the hook, he had the propensity to overload that compartment on every trip.

One day, after returning from the Caribbean Island of Dominica, another load was ready to be put aboard and flown to St. Thomas. After asking Manuel to leave access to the hook, we went to lunch. Returning to the aircraft, he greeted us, smiling while handing me the load manifest.

"Did you leave me access to the shepherd's hook?" I asked.

"Si, Captain. I show you."

Climbing aboard the aircraft, much to my frustration and dismay, I discovered the 'J' compartment loaded to the max with the hook invisible and unreachable. "Dammit, Manuel! How many times do I have to tell you that I need to be able to reach the hook at all times?"

"Captain, please follow me. You will see, there is no problem."

Manuel entered the cockpit and stood, pointing to the hook lying across the bench jump seat.

"See!" he said. "Now, whenever you need it, it is here. Why do you never think of dis?"

Something else I never thought of: why didn't I ever tell him WHY I needed access to the bloody hook?

Another lesson learned!

Chapter Five
"THE FATAL CRASH OF ROBERTO CLEMENTE"

Douglas DC-7

Roberto Clemente

I enjoyed San Juan, PR, and flying to many of the Caribbean Islands as a new C-46 captain for Shamrock Airlines. It was one of many non-scheduled airlines operating from Ypsilanti, MI. After joining the company, I was sent almost immediately to their temporary San Juan base, servicing the British and American Virgin Islands, Haiti, the Dominican Republic, and Jamaica.

A DC-3 based on the field was operated and owned by Arthur Rivera. Arthur, a native Puerto Rican, enjoyed very little freight competition until Shamrock Airlines arrived. Deciding he needed more 'lift' capability, Arthur purchased a DC-7 aircraft that he found rusting at 'Corrosion Corner' in Miami. It was not in the best condition, and after several days of serious maintenance to get it somewhat flyable, a crew was found willing to ferry it to San Juan, Puerto Rico. It languished for several weeks on a closed taxiway of the San Juan Airport, as daily maintenance was performed by Arthur's DC-3 mechanics, never making even one flight.

2 Shamrock Airlines C-46 aircraft on the ramp at San Juan, Puerto Rico.

On December 7, Arthur received a call from the airport authority requesting he move the plane from the closed taxiway. Not having a crew available to move the aircraft, he took that task upon himself.

Barely qualified as a DC-3 co-pilot, he was not even qualified to start the engines on the 7' but somehow managed to start numbers one and four.

Signaling for the wheel chalks to be removed, the aircraft immediately started rolling. Facing in the correct direction, it accelerated rapidly as it approached the end of the taxiway. A right or left turn was required to prevent crashing into a concrete, water-filled drainage ditch at the end of the taxiway. Unfortunately, the hydraulic power on the DC-7 came from the left and right inboard engines (usually engine positions #2 and #3, counting from left to right). These engines operated the hydraulic pumps that powered various systems on the aircraft, including the flight controls, landing gear, and brakes. The outboard engines (positions #1 and #4) did not have dedicated hydraulic pumps to power the systems. Instead, the hydraulic systems primarily relied on the inboard engines. Hydraulic power was distributed throughout the aircraft via a network of reservoirs and lines.

The aircraft had no braking or nose wheel steering, so it quickly came to rest in the concrete-filled drainage ditch. Significant damage was sustained to all four propellers. Engine damage from the two operating engines at the time of the incident was also suspected but never seriously investigated. Eventually, the aircraft was extracted from the ditch and spent a few more weeks in maintenance, where all four propellers were replaced.

The engines were later run for a few hours, but never inspected for damage beyond the engine runs.

On December 23, 1972, Managua, Nicaragua, suffered a 6.2 magnitude earthquake. I received a call from Arthur, who mentioned that he had heard I was a former co-pilot on the DC-7. "Would you be interested in co-piloting my '7' on several relief flights to Managua?" he asked.

Explaining that I was busy flying the C-46s and was in no way professionally current to do so, I turned him down. Not taking no for an answer, he mentioned that a 'celebrity' client was chartering the DC-7 and paying exceptionally well. He refused to name the celebrity when asked. He noted that the person was paying for several relief flights, and I could make a bundle. Refusing again, I thanked him for the offer and ended the call.

Below is the report of that first and only fateful flight. There, but for the grace of God...Etc. Etc.

The Report:

Roberto Clemente was both a remarkable ballplayer and a genuine folk hero. As an outfielder for the Pittsburgh Pirates, Clemente was a perennial All-Star and Gold Glove recipient.

On December 23, 1972, a 6.2-magnitude earthquake rocked Managua, Nicaragua. Some 5,000 people lost their lives, another 20,000 were injured, and over 250,000 were displaced from their homes.

Swayed by his recent time in Nicaragua, Clemente coordinated an extraordinary effort to provide emergency supplies to the victims. Despite sending three airplane loads to Managua, supplies still needed to be flown to Nicaragua.

Arthur Rivera approached Clemente and offered his DC-7 cargo plane to airlift the remaining relief supplies. Clemente inspected the plane and agreed to pay Rivera $4000 (approximately $22,000 today) upon his return to Puerto Rico.

By law, Rivera was to provide a pilot, co-pilot, and flight engineer. Rivera hired a pilot, Jerry Hill, and appointed himself the co-pilot despite his lack of certification to co-pilot the DC-7. He had been unable to employ a flight engineer for the flight.

Unbeknownst to Clemente, the DC-7 had been involved in that unreported incident on December 2, 1972, when a loss of hydraulic power caused the aircraft to leave the taxiway and crash into a water-filled concrete ditch. (Mentioned above.) After the incident, an airworthiness inspector with the Federal Aviation

Administration (FAA) questioned Rivera about intended repairs to the plane. Mr. Rivera confirmed that he intended to repair the aircraft, but the inspector took no further action.

After that, the damaged propellers were replaced, and the engines were run for three hours, showing no signs of malfunction. The repairmen returned the airplane to service; however, the FAA did not inspect it before the ill-fated flight. The plane had not even been flown since its arrival from Miami in September 1972.

The loading of Rivera's DC-7 was completed on December 31, 1972. Clemente decided to personally accompany this flight after being advised that their prior shipments may not have reached the intended recipients due to governmental interference with the relief efforts.

The flight plan was filed with the FAA on the morning of December 31st. At approximately 9:11 pm, the flight taxied down Runway 7 and was cleared for takeoff.

The weather was good, and visibility was 10 miles. The first takeoff attempt was aborted, and no reason was given.

Upon the successful second takeoff, the plane gained minimal altitude, and at 9:23 pm, the tower received a message that the plane was turning back around. Unfortunately, the aircraft did not make it, crashing into the Atlantic Ocean about one and a half miles from shore. Everyone aboard the plane, including Roberto Clemente, perished in the crash. He was just 38 years old.

The post-occurrence investigation revealed that an engine had failed before the crash and that the plane was nearly 4200 pounds over the maximum allowable gross takeoff weight.

Resulting Lawsuit:

Vera Zabala Clemente and the next of kin of the other passengers filed a lawsuit against the United States of America, alleging that the FAA employees were negligent under the Federal Tort Claims Act and responsible for the resulting crash.

(The Federal Tort Claims Act is a limited waiver of sovereign immunity that authorizes parties to sue the United States for tortious conduct.)

Factually, the plaintiffs' claim was based on the premise that the FAA owed a duty to promote flight safety, which was breached by its failure to revoke the DC-7's airworthiness certificate after the December 2, 1972, accident, monitor the repair process, and otherwise discover that the plane was not airworthy, had an improper registration number, was not properly weighted and balanced, and did not have a qualified crew.

The plaintiff argued that had the FAA acted under its internal procedures (Order SO8430.20C, "Continuous Surveillance of Large and Turbine Powered Aircraft"), the aircraft would have been denied flight clearance, the deceased passengers would have been advised of the deficiencies, and the plane crash would never have happened.

The United States countered that the FAA had no legal duty towards the decedents to "discover or anticipate acts which might result in a violation of Federal Regulations." They also claimed that there was no connection between any duty and the fatal crash.

Who Won?

The trial court found in favor of Vera Zabala Clemente and the next of kin of the other deceased passengers on the issue of negligence.

Why?

The FAA investigative report convinced the trial court that the cause of the crash was 'overboosting' of the No. 2 engine at takeoff and that the plane was overloaded by more than two tons.

Because the flight crew was inadequate, the situation was such that "...for all practical purposes, the Captain was flying solo in emergency conditions."

Section 6 of Order SO8430.20C called for "continuous surveillance of large and turbine-powered aircraft to determine noncompliance of Federal Aviation Regulations." Furthermore, a ramp inspection would now be required to determine that the crew and operator complied with the safety requirements regarding the airworthiness of the aircraft, including the weight, balance, and pilot qualifications. Any indication of an "illegal" flight crew was to be made known to the crew and persons chartering the service. Finally, discovering such noncompliance was prioritized, second only to accident investigation.

The trial court found that the Continuous Surveillance of Large and Turbine Powered Aircraft order provisions applied to Roberto Clemente's chartered flight and that the decedents were within the class of people who sought to be protected under the order. If the required ramp inspection had been completed, the lack of a proper crew and overloading would have been discovered, Clemente would have been notified, and he would not have agreed to board the plane and avoided his untimely death.

The order was held to be mandatory, and because the FAA violated its orders, a failure to exercise due care was evident.

Accordingly, the FAA's failure to inspect and ground the plane "contributed to the death of the...decedents." There were five souls on board. Four bodies were later recovered. Roberto Clemente's body has never been found.

Chapter Six
"JUST ANOTHER THURSDAY"

Hansa Jet

It was the 1970s. Returning from San Juan, I discovered several jet charter companies offering a myriad of jet aircraft for charter. Soon, Netjets, Bizjet, or JetLinx would join the mix; Zantop Airways was among the first.

Lloyd Zantop, formerly of Zantop Air Transport, my former employer, re-hired me to fly a Hansa Jet. He had started a jet operation at Detroit Metro Airport, utilizing Learjet and Hansa Jet aircraft. I was soon upgraded to a Hansa Jet captain.

As one of the duty crew, I was awakened early by flight dispatch on a dreary, rainy Thursday morning. "Please get here ASAP," a voice said. "The aircraft has already been fueled. You are scheduled to meet on an Olympic Airlines flight arriving at JFK from Athens at noon.

You will have 6 or 7 passengers. Destination: Rochester, MN. (KRST) The primary passenger is an ill Greek tycoon. He is traveling with his support staff of valets, assistants, a chef, and medical personnel. From JFK, file the flight plan as a MedEvac flight to KRST. Hurry, please."

On arrival at the airport, I was handed a 'flight packet' stating, among other things, Olympic Airlines operations discreet ground control frequency to be called when fifteen or twenty minutes from landing. "They will provide you gate arrival info for the flight you will meet. Instructions will be issued on the ground so you can park next to the aircraft for passenger pickup."

I remember thinking: *This guy must be terribly ill or have a lot of juice (Position of Authority) for this kind of priority.* My co-pilot for the day was Charlie Atterbury. He was a competent, no-nonsense guy. With a very dry wit, he could always be counted on to lighten any moment, regardless of the circumstances, while getting the job done.

Living much closer, Charlie preceded me to the airport, completed the walk-around inspection, filed the flight plan, and stocked coffee, water, and galley incidentals for immediate departure. Upon arrival, I was briefed on the terrible in-flight weather we could expect. We were soon airborne.

Deviating several miles from the course to avoid the many TRWs associated with an occluded weather front across our flight route put us behind our scheduled arrival at JFK.

When we contacted Olympic Operations with our ETA, we were informed that the flight we were to meet had just landed. Asked to expedite, we were given gate and parking instructions to be passed on to JFK Ground Control.

An ILS approach to minimums, perhaps a bit below minimums, was made to Rwy31 left. Arriving at the gate, we were directed to park well behind the right wing of the Boeing 747. Almost immediately, an Olympic ground vehicle arrived with baggage and passengers—seven pax with a mountain of baggage. Charlie saw to the refuelling while I struggled with the baggage, catering, passengers, and rain, which was now pouring down in torrents.

The lead passenger was introduced to us as Mr. Kosmo Lagana. (Charlie immediately began referring to him irreverently as 'Mr. Cosmic Lasagna.') Two very burly Olympic Airline employees carried Mr. Lagana off the Boeing down a set of air stairs, pushed against the rear door of the Boeing, and then gently into our aircraft.

We were informed he could walk, but only with difficulty, considering possible and unlikely evacuation procedures. We were advised that the Mayo Clinic ambulance would be standing by to take Mr. Lagana immediately to the hospital upon our arrival at KRST. While airborne, we made a sky-phone call to the Mayo, advising them of our ETA.

Due to headwinds and storm deviations, we were about 45 minutes beyond our scheduled arrival time.

Mr. Lagana's valet, Stavros, approached the cockpit several times during the flight. When asked how things were in the back and how he was doing, his response was always: "Just another Thursday."

Finding that a rather odd response, Charlie asked, "Are they all the same for you?"

"Pretty much," came the reply. It seemed to us that he was pretty bored.

During the ensuing conversation, I noticed that our fuel gauges were wrong or we were burning much more fuel than planned. Not wishing to alarm Stavros, I casually mentioned that I needed Charlie for a moment: "Could we talk later, please?"

As he left the cockpit, I said, "Houston, I think we have a problem," pointing to the fuel gauges.

Charlie's response left no doubt: "Holy Shit!"

Switching from tank-to-tank indications and checking engine parameters, the engines appeared to operate normally. What could it be? We were going to be lucky to make it to KRST. We should have had a few hours of reserve fuel on arrival, but now, everything seemed doubtful. Because of CG and gross weight takeoff requirements, we had almost full fuel tanks departing JFK. However, we did have enough for a missed approach, an alternate airport fuel requirement, and about an hour on arrival at KRST.

Immediately reducing power and speed to long-range cruise performance, Charlie quickly calculated that we would make KRST, but just precluded any missed approach. Flying well above an overcast sky, we advised ATC of our predicament and requested the nearest accommodating airports if needed. (This was well before such amenities as modern-day Flight Management Systems.) Climbing to FL 410 helped reduce the fuel flow indications. Staying as high as possible, as long as possible, ATC was more than accommodating. Eventually, handing us off to KRST approach control during a rapid descent through ten thousand feet, we were immediately cleared for an ILS approach to Rwy31.

As we touched down, we both breathed an audible sigh of relief. The fuel gauges had nearly read empty. Arriving on the ramp, the Mayo Clinic ambulance and several limos pulled up to the aircraft. Charlie opened the door and, within seconds, grabbed my arm and attention. "Skippy, we are pissing a hell of a lot of fuel out of the hell hole vent." (The hell hole hatch is to access the aircraft's hell hole or belly.)

"Keep everyone away from the back of the aircraft. Divert their attention somehow. I will do the same."

Fortunately, 'Mr. Cosmic Lasagna' and no other passengers saw or heard the fuel splashing as it ran from the aircraft's belly, except the valet, Stavros.

"What is that running from the aircraft?" he wanted to know.

Charlie, quick as ever, said: "That? Oh, that, you see, these are older generation engines that have not been modified to collect the unburned fuel as the engines are secured. They are scheduled for the upgrade this week." Adding "Just another Thursday" with a smile.

Skeptical, he stepped into the limo and was heard saying, "Seems like a heck of a lot of unburned fuel!"

Dropping the 'hell hole' hatch, we were splashed with jet fuel. The entire belly was filled with fuel, resting between the fuselage stringers. Opening or checking the 'hell hole' at JFK was not routine, especially as it was raining heavily, or this anomaly would have been discovered sooner. Either there had not been sufficient fuel accumulation in the belly then, or due to the torrential downpour, fuel leaking from the belly was just missed. What is that old saying about Murphy's Law?

The Hansa Jet aircraft had two large rotary inverters in the belly. When selected, they were known to produce a spark occasionally. Fortunately for us, that did not happen. This was the aircraft's first flight after a major inspection. A close static inspection found nothing that could have caused this tremendous fuel leak. Refueled with the engines started, a maintenance tech placed himself in the belly and soon found the problem, as the engines were run at cruise power. The inverters were not switched on.

It was discovered that a fuel line bracket that kept the line from chaffing due to vibration against a fuselage stringer had either broken or had never been properly attached. A hole had been rubbed in the line. Under pressure, fuel spewed out of that hole in copious amounts. Not enough to cause an engine flame-out, just enough to dangerously fill the belly, venting the excess overboard. The earlier rough ride to JFK due to TRW turbulence and an equally turbulent ride to KRST as the jet stream wandered sporadically across our flight path contributed in no small way to the size of that hole.

No doubt a poor design, the aircraft was soon modified, repaired, test-flown, and returned to service. The FAA was notified, and an AD (Airworthiness Directive) was issued.

We later learned that 'Mr. Cosmic Lasagna' expired soon after arriving at Mayo. At least we were not responsible for his demise.

"Just another Thursday?" Nope, not really.

Chapter Seven
"ADRIFT IN ADRENALINE"

Viper engine-powered Hawker 1A

Nordo Express!

Readers of my book, *Flying Vagabond*, may recall that when the Hansa Jet aircraft, which we had been sharing flight time and expenses with Pepsi Bottling of Miami after Zantop, became unavailable due to court action, an older Hawker jet aircraft was found to replace it. It was leased from McCollum Aviation, an aircraft broker from Danville, IL. It was agreed that the plane would be delivered, and all leasing transactions would be finalized and signed at Combs-Gates FBO in Indianapolis, Indiana.

Arriving from Miami, our flight was held for 40 minutes before a landing approach could be commenced due to a thunderstorm passing over the field. We finally touched down when the weather was at a landing minimum amid heavy rain showers. A telephone call was made to Combs-Gates requesting a ride to their facility. Inquiring whether our expected Hawker had arrived yet, we were informed they had radioed advising they were twenty minutes out.

Arriving at the FBO, a pair of aircraft landing lights were seen appearing through the overcast and landing. This was our expected Hawker jet. An incredible engine screech preceded its arrival on the aircraft ramp. This was an early model British Hawker 400, which used early-generation engines called Vipers. They should have been called Banshees. Without ear protection, one would likely suffer permanent hearing damage with prolonged exposure to the engine whine.

The engines were finally secured, throwing the aircraft ramp into a welcome silence. The plane's door slowly opened a minute later, and an angular figure exited. His hair was cropped close to his scalp, and he was unshaven. He wore old baggy jeans and cowboy boots with a very rumpled cowboy-style shirt that appeared as though it was from a Goodwill grab bag. Carrying a briefcase, he extended his hand and introduced himself as 'Whatcha McCollum.' "You can call me Whatchy."

His real first name was Louis, but no one ever called him that, if they knew it. He enjoyed a reputation in aviation basically as a pilot broker who dealt in older, often barely flyable aircraft. Those who knew him and his reputation avoided doing business with him. We were soon to find out why!

Hesitating while looking toward the aircraft, we were expecting to see another pilot step out. Whatcha said, "What are we waiting for?"

"Your other pilot to join us," I said.

"There is no other pilot aboard. I flew it here myself. It's an easy airplane to fly, as you will see."

Stunned, all we could say was, "Oh!"

He went on to say, "I even washed it off for you. I flew it through that thunderstorm that just crossed the field."

Another, "Oh," while casting a sideways glance at each other.

Entering the FBO, Whatchy proceeded to procure a rental car for a one-way rental back to Danville. At the same time, we silently made a mental note to look the aircraft over well before departing for Miami. Money was soon wired, contracts signed, and we climbed aboard after a thorough walk-around completed by both of us. The aircraft seemed ancient, with a threadbare interior that had seen many better days. We also noticed a peculiar musty odor that one wouldn't expect from a corporate jet. Mentioning this, Whatcha said that the plane hadn't flown "in a while" but, as soon as fresh air is introduced, it will "hardly be noticeable."

The cockpit was filthy, with black rings surrounding many of the most frequently used switches.

The instrument gauges had so many finger smudges on them that they required a thorough cleaning even before the engine started. Everything was filthy. Pointing out the sad state of the interior, McCollum shrugged, saying, "A little Windex and upholstery cleaner would spruce things up in no time."

He was the lessor. We wondered why he didn't try to make a reasonable first impression. Upon reflection, his state of dress should have screamed, 'Beware.' The odyssey was about to begin.

I was not captain-qualified in the Hawker jet and had never flown one. My first officer from the Hansa Jet days, however, did hold a captain's type rating in the Hawker, which was the determinant of leasing one. He claimed to have a lot of time in a Hawker—I later discovered he had only about 15 hours in type. He had taken his type rating in a Hawker 400F with Fan-Jet engines and had never seen an old Viper-powered Hawker. He was barely current but legally qualified to fly one since all Hawker types were one-type rating. (What is wrong with that picture?)

The liability was mounting almost as high as my blood pressure. I had taken my first officer's word for it. Holy crap, what had I gotten myself into? It was a hard lesson well learned. Thank God for checklists. Reading the 'Before Start Engine Checklist' and observing my F/O stumble and search for switches whose very names seemed a mystery to him almost had me reaching for the door. In retrospect, I should have. Strike One!

Approximately thirty minutes later, the engines finally started, and all checklists were completed up to the 'Taxi Checklist.' Taxi clearance was requested and received. Finally moving off the ramp, I noticed ground control was barely readable. The #1 radio was in use, so I switched to #2. It was even worse. Switching back to number one, my F/O said that the #2 radio antenna was on the bottom of the aircraft, which was why it was almost unreadable. Okay, but why was number one nearly unreadable if its antenna was on top of the aircraft? Strike Two!

Reaching the end of the runway, takeoff clearance was received, and we were at last airborne with trepidation to Miami. Switching from departure control to enroute radar, we were given an unrestricted climb to FL350 (thirty-five thousand feet). The radio signals had not improved on either radio, with all transmissions scratchy and almost unreadable. Apprehensively, we settled in for a long flight. Heading south and away from the weather, it was a star-studded night with smooth air and a steady wind. At times, communication with ATC was scratchy but readable. Soon, however, noticing a prolonged period of radio silence, I called ATC for a radio check. No reply. After attempting several times with #1 radio, we switched to #2. There was no reply after several attempts with that, either.

The radio rack in the Hawker, I was told, was located under the forward baggage compartment. Leaving the cockpit, I removed the radio rack cover and reseated all the radios.

Numbers one and two radios had yellow repair tags, and the dates were over three years old. OMG! Like everything else in this beast, they were worn out. Reseating the transponder, I hoped it was working. It also had a yellow tag, but its date was much more recent. It was only a little over a year out of check. I climbed back into the cockpit and attempted to contact ATC or any airborne aircraft that could relay for us. No luck. I set the transponder to squawk 7600, the radio failure code, and hoped it worked. We were now NORDO (No Radio). Strike Three! (Some smaller general aviation aircraft are not equipped with two-way communications radios. These are generally small single- or two-seat tandem aircraft. Pilots who fly these often carry portable radio gear to remain in contact with the ground. When a more complex aircraft is referred to as NORDO, it implies that the installed audio gear has ceased to function for some reason and is no longer in contact with anyone on the ground or in the air.)

A discussion ensued as to the correct procedure to follow in this event. It was agreed that we had been cleared to Miami via the flight plan filed earlier and should adhere to it. Tension and adrenaline were maxed out as we were unsure if our transponder code was being received or still in radar contact. Of course, we were, but all sorts of scenarios ran through my head. My "captain" was borderline catatonic, which did not help the situation. I took control of the aircraft and told him to take a break and a few deep breaths.

I intended to descend from altitude at four times our distance from Miami, as we had a pretty good tailwind.

As we reached that point, I commenced a descent. With the speed increasing, I gently reduced the power on both engines.

Both engines immediately compressor stalled with the ITTs (Internal Turbine Temp) increasing rapidly. Restoring the power levers very gently mitigated the compressor stalls but left us with too much power. Attempting once again to reduce power slowly, one engine at a time, also resulted in an engine stall, but I found that the engine would eventually recover. The ITTs returned to normal gradually, but increased every time throttle movement was made rapidly in either direction. The banging from the engines as the compressors stalled was, to say the least, disconcerting.

At this point, I thought I would surely lose my inexperienced captain/co-pilot. The movie 'The High And The Mighty' came to mind, in which John Wayne was the co-pilot of a DC-4 en route from Hawaii to SFO, with Robert Stack as the captain. The captain started to lose it, so John Wayne reached over and slapped him hard, yelling, "Snap out of it." That would be appropriate. Let's see. I believe that was Strike Four!

I soon mastered engine management. Now, we face the problem of landing safely. I knew of the tower's light signals available for such emergencies, but had never experienced them. Green was always good, but I remembered alternating red and green meant something else. But what?

It did not matter because I was landing no matter what. This bird was sick. We entered about a five-mile final for Rwy 9L at Miami. The tower must have known we were coming as we got a green light followed by an alternating red and green light, which, we found out later, was "Cleared to land. Proceed with caution."

Arriving at the Associated Aircraft ramp, the FAA met us to inspect our certificates and the lease paperwork. The inspector took McCollum's information, notified him, and asked him to provide maintenance records. In the meantime, I called British Aerospace, the aircraft manufacturer, to tell them about the engine stalls and get information on where the aircraft should be inspected. When asked for the aircraft serial number, I was told that that aircraft no longer existed. Wait, what?

The British rep said that the aircraft we were flying had been wrecked several years before in a runway overrun accident in Haleyville, Ala. It was totaled and removed from their records. He went on to say that British Aerospace had heard that it was repaired illegally against the manufacturer's advice. The call ended with a "Good Luck" sign-off!

An engine shop was on the field, and the engines were repaired. We also had the radios repaired and re-certified by Collins Avionics at MIA and billed to McCollum. The lease would eventually be canceled, but not before I was granted permission to use the aircraft to acquire a Hawker-type rating.

I studied the manual, took an oral exam, and took a check ride from an FAA examiner who had never been in a Hawker; he was a check pilot primarily on Saberliner aircraft. The oral exam and check ride were a piece of cake.

My F/O and I eventually moved on to other employment. We had heard that the CEO of Pepsi Bottling filed a lawsuit against McCollum. I was never informed of the result. Several years later, while flying for Lloyd Zantop in Detroit, Whatchy asked me to check him out in a Hansa Jet he had just acquired. I turned him down. Not long after, we heard that he had been killed at a small airport in Michigan while flying a Hansa. The Hansa Jet liked long runways. McCollum used the short one, overran it, and was killed. I have since acquired over nine thousand hours in many different Hawker models.

A memorable takeaway: never fly an "A Model" of anything! As the saying goes, "You never forget your first one!"

Chapter Eight
"GETTING OUT ALIVE"

Nicolae Ceausescu's Romania

Returning from Africa late at night from a long and adventurous sojourn to the Dark Continent, I decided to stay in bed and read after an excellent room service breakfast. This was a few years after many short-term adventures with Shamrock, Zantop, and Pepsi Bottling of Miami. The English International CNN reported the local weather in Athens as sunny, with a high layer of broken clouds. The temperature was said to be low at 40°F. Looking out from my hotel window, the Parthenon on the Athenian Acropolis was illuminated in the brilliant sunshine. Happy to be back in the 'Cradle of Democracy' and exhausted, I wanted nothing to do with airplanes for at least a day or so.

As many of the Flying Vagabond readers may remember, the Africa trip was memorable. Landing in Khartoum, Sudan, without clearance, out of necessity because of low fuel, proved more than problematic. This resulted in our brief incarceration, which endured the most unpleasant and frightful of circumstances. Our survival depended on the goodwill of the Sudanese military, who were our jailers. Fortunately, one of my passengers at the time was a United States senator. Discovering this, our jailers became noticeably less belligerent.

Khartoum had always been a good 'technical' stop for aircraft transiting into or out of the Dark Continent. On this particular occasion, we were unaware that Ethiopia, Sudan's archenemy, had launched an offensive into Sudan that morning. The country was at war, and we landed in the middle. Happily, because of the US senator and the US embassy staff, we were released with a promise not to return anytime soon. No Problem!

A hot shower and a delicious room service breakfast set the plan for the day: relaxation and recovery. It had been a very hectic few days. Well, that was the plan, but the best-laid plans, etc.

The phone rang; it was Aladdin, the aircraft's owner, and my boss.

"Captain Edie, could we leave later today for Bucharest?" (He never got my name right despite my several attempts telling him it was EDDIE, not EDIE. Oh well.)

"What time did you have in mind?"

"Well, we only just arrived back in Athens several hours ago. However, I urgently need to travel to Romania. Please make preparations."

(Bucharest, Romania, was another first for me. All I knew of the country was where Dracula lived, if you pardon the pun.) "So, I guess you want to leave ASAP?"

"Yes! Please call me when everything is ready for our departure. Only my four brothers and I will be traveling, and we will be staying the night. I have already made reservations for you at a nice hotel in the city center."

I woke Roger from a deep sleep with the good news. "You gotta be shittin' me! The freaking engines haven't even cooled yet."

"I'm not kidding; I wish I were. Have you ever been there?"

"Hell no! That's a Commie country, for Christ's sake. How are we supposed to do this?"

"I haven't a clue, but get yourself ready. We will be spending the night if we can even pull this off. While you prepare, I am calling Universal WX for permits and a flight plan. I will meet you in the lobby in 30 minutes."

Universal informed me that getting overflight permits from Bulgaria and landing permission from the Romanians may take a while.

"Bulgaria? Just where the hell is that?" I asked.

"North of Greece. You have to overfly it to get to Romania. Give me an hour. I will 'Twixt' Athens Aviation with your info." (A Twix is an old technology that is no longer used in our modern age. This was 1977.)

A quick call to Athens Aviation requesting the usual catering, fuel, etc., and we were soon on our way. Bessie, Athens Aviation gal Friday, and my Athenian tour guide were waiting. Looking sad, I asked if anything was wrong.

"Not wrong, just disappointed. I was going to surprise you. I am off in an hour and was coming to your hotel. Ah, shucks! That would have been a hell of a lot more fun than visiting the Commies."

"I'll be back tomorrow. Hold that thought."

She smiled as she handed me our international flight plan with an overflight number for Bulgaria and a landing permission number for Bucharest. That didn't take long at all. Amazing!

After fueling, coffee, catering, and ice were on board, a call to Aladdin brought them to the airport in twenty minutes. The flight was uneventful. Looking down as we traversed Bulgaria, it appeared a 'Third World Country,' seriously underdeveloped, bleak, and uninviting. I wondered what Romania was like. Passing overhead Golyama VOR, the last fix in Bulgaria, we were instructed to contact Romanian Radar. We were immediately given headings to fly to keep us away from potentially restricted areas.

The instrument approach and landing in Bucharest were uneventful despite the poor visibility. After contacting 'ground control,' we were directed to a vast ramp devoid of aircraft or vehicles. We were told to stay on the plane and monitor the ground control frequency for further instructions.

About fifteen minutes passed when a military-looking vehicle approached, stopping near the aircraft. Twelve uniformed and heavily armed men alighted from the back of the car. Falling into formation, they marched toward and stopped at the aircraft's wing. We had been informing Aladdin of these goings, but we weren't quite ready for this reception!

"What is happening?" Roger asked.

Trying to remain calm, I said, "How should I know? Maybe we are getting special handling because we have an American flag painted on the tail."

The ground controller then transmitted that we were cleared to deplane and to provide the officer in charge with our passports.

As we opened the door, what appeared to be a limo pulled up for the passengers. Aladdin climbed on board and yelled that he knew where we were staying and would be in touch. Well, okay then!

After handing our passports to the guy who seemed in charge, we secured the aircraft. When we were finished, we were escorted to a military vehicle and driven to the terminal building. It turned out that a security detail was placed around the aircraft—at least, that was what I hoped.

The bloody terminal building was vast and empty except for about ten or twelve uniformed people, with several uniformed women among them. Our suitcases were taken from us and placed on an X-ray machine. I had a pistol-shaped hair dryer, which caused much chatter. Indeed, thankfully, they had seen one of those before. We were escorted to a secluded, curtained area where a heavy-set and not unattractive young lady stood. She motioned that I should proceed behind the curtain with her following. This turned out to be a cubicle with drawn curtains on all sides.

Standing there and wondering what happened, this young lady patted me down. She rubbed her hands everywhere, on my ass, my crotch, which she gently squeezed, all the while looking me in the eye and smiling. She stuck her hand down the back of my trousers. Jesus, if I had not been so apprehensive about where we were, this might have been fun. When she finished, she smiled, patted me on the cheek, and opened the curtain. Roger stepped from the other cubicle with the guy who checked him. He said, "I have just been molested!"

"So have I," I said, pointing to the woman who had just had her hand in my pants.

"You lucky bastard," he said.

We were escorted to the front of the building, where we retrieved our luggage and were handed our passports. A car and driver were waiting. The driver spoke broken English.

He welcomed us to the Peoples Republic or some shit like that and said he knew where we were staying. Hmm.

Everything seemed colorless and worn. Very few people were seen on our drive through the city. The buildings were in an ancient European style, and many crumbled with more than a few broken windows. It was winter, and it was freezing. It had recently snowed. There was a visible 'haze' in the air. I did not know what it was, but we had also noticed it on our approach to landing. Pollution, I guess. That would account for the funny smell.

Checking in at the hotel was a non-event despite the language difficulty. The hotel was old and smelled funny, as did the city. (Nowadays, Marriott, Hilton, and Radisson all have hotels there.) My room was something out of the late 1800s. A pair of ugly chandeliers hung low overhead in the hallway and the main room. They were on and giving off an eerie yellowish glow. It was approaching dusk, and daylight was beginning to fade. The bathroom had a shower, which was the entire bathroom. A spigot stuck out from the wall, and a drain was in the center of the floor for the runoff.

There were two pictures of the Romanian President, Nicolae Ceaușescu, on the walls: one in the hallway and a larger one in the main room. Rogers's room was as spartan as mine. We both thought we had 'time-traveled.' There was no restaurant in the hotel.

We were directed to go to what was promised to be 'perfect' just down the street. While walking toward the restaurant, we were approached by a twenty-five-year-old man who had stepped from a darkened doorway, frightening both of us. Tugging my arm, he tried to direct me toward the same doorway. I resisted. He whispered in English: "Americans, do you have US dollars to sell?"

I guess we stood out, or perhaps something more nefarious was happening. Athens Aviation had warned me to be extremely careful of the Romanian secret police, as they were watching everyone. *Who was this guy? Secret police?* I was unsure. I wouldn't do such a thing anyway. We pushed past him and kept walking. It was pretty strange looking back on it, as he seemed to be the only other person on the street except for us. Weird place!

The restaurant was as drab as the rest of the city. The tablecloth had stains, and the waiter's excuse for a Tux was threadbare and stained. We ordered fish, which was not bad. Paying the check later, I tried to leave a tip. Through sign language, the waiter advised us that it was unnecessary, as that was not expected or accepted in his country. Arriving back at the hotel, I decided to try calling my kids in Florida. I would probably wake them, but I missed them. Dialing the hotel operator, I was advised that she spoke no English. "Est-ce-que tu parles Francais?" (Do you speak French?) she asked.

"Nope! Sprichst du Deutsch?" (Do you speak German?) I asked.

"Ja," she said.

Being a little conversant in German from my younger school days in Germany, I asked if it would be possible to call the US. She said yes, but the service could be better and may take some time. I gave her my info, hung up, and waited. Thirty minutes later, she called me back and told me to stand by. After one or two minutes, I heard the voices of my family. It was a little scratchy, but it was good. While talking with my wife, I sneezed. A female voice said: "GESUNDHEIT!"

"Who was that?" my then-wife demanded.

The hotel operator was listening to our conversation. I wasn't sure if that was necessary, but I became very wary of anything I might say derogatory about Bucharest.

Later, hanging up and noticing it was stifling hot in the room, I opened a window, as there was no thermostat anywhere. I lay on the bed and saw a thin haze wafting through the window. It held my attention as it filled the room. It had that same odor I had smelled since arriving in this God-forsaken place. Closing the window and lying on the bed, I wondered if the Learjet was okay. No TV, poor yellowish lighting, no books to read, and gray people made me especially appreciate Western civilization and the US of A. Gad! What a place to live.

I couldn't help but feel sorry for the people living under this or any communist regime. Approximately 12 years later, Ceaușescu was executed along with his wife, Elena, after being tried and convicted by the people he had so long oppressed and abused. He was found guilty of genocide, murdering over 60,000 of his people. One hundred twenty bullets were found in their bodies. Do you think they were pissed off?

After a fitful night's sleep, I received a call from Aladdin. We were to leave in three hours to return to Athens. Thank God! I called Universal, which took almost an hour and advised them of our departure. As we prepared to leave the hotel, the desk clerk handed me our flight plan, a new overflight permit for Bulgaria, route weather, and 'Notams' (Notices to Airmen). Universal Weather and Aviation, based in Houston, TX, proved worth every penny of their fee. They made us look good every day we flew!

Arriving at the airport, I had hoped to see that chubby little lady who so gently caressed my crotch, but she was nowhere in sight. We handed our passports to a uniformed official in the near-empty terminal building, who stamped and returned them. We were then driven out to our Learjet. Six soldiers were placed around the aircraft, guarding it. Guarding it from what I don't know, but I was happy to see them.

Alighting from the vehicle and approaching the aircraft, someone stopped us. I presumed that it was the officer in charge of the guard detail.

He asked again for our passports and stood behind us as we opened the aircraft door. Sitting on the potty seat and in plain view of the officer was a whole carton of Marlboro cigarettes that I used as baksheesh (bribe) when needed during our travels. He motioned toward the cigarettes while imitating smoking. It was clear he wanted a pack. Asking for the return of our passports, I opened the carton and handed him a pack. He motioned again for more, looking at his soldiers standing in formation and semi-attention. Long story short, he ended up with the whole carton. I'll just bet he is still smiling!

After passengers arrived and clearances were received, we left Bucharest and never returned. Bessie was waiting!

Chapter Nine
"IMPERFECT PITCH!"

Not long after returning to the States, I needed a job. I soon received a call from a person who identified himself as Mr. Murphy, the owner of Bimini Island Airways in Fort Lauderdale. He mentioned a mutual friend had given him my name. Hearing I was an experienced Hawker jet pilot, he explained he had just refurbished, painted, and sold a Hawker jet he had owned for a couple of years. The aircraft's new owner was a US citizen and a noted Ft. Lauderdale eye surgeon originally from the Dominican Republic. I was informed that the doctor was anxious to take delivery. He explained further that some maintenance had been done on the aircraft, and a test flight was required. He needed a familiar and current Hawker pilot. Was I available? After further discussion, an agreement was reached.

Arriving at FXE (Fort Lauderdale Executive Airport) a few days later, introductions were made, temporary employment contracts signed, and a walkout to the Hawker followed a tour of the facility. Approaching the jet, the sun reflected a silken sheen to its newly painted surface. I noticed it was a much older 600-model Hawker jet, one in which I had a good deal of experience. The original Viper engines had been replaced with newer Garrett 731 Fan-Jet engines. The aircraft was parked in an unused area of the large ramp, which I found odd. It was the only jet aircraft on the property and seemed hidden away from sight. Bimini Island Airways operated only two aircraft: a Swearingen Metro liner and a Saab 340 turboprop aircraft, but no jets.

Knowing the aircraft's age, I could not wait to get inside. Murphy stated it had been painted outside and had a new cabin interior. As we approached, I asked if the cockpit avionics had been upgraded.

"No, that would have added more money and time to the sale," indicating the doctor was interested in quick delivery. He sheepishly added, "She's a good airplane."

The remark struck me as odd, evoking a silent note of caution. I wondered why he would say that. Generally, all aircraft of that class are considered good airplanes. I determined that long before I took this aircraft airborne, it would behoove me to give her an excellent and thorough preflight inspection. I was about to discover the wisdom of that reasoning.

"When was it last flown?" I asked.

His reply startled me. "It hasn't flown for two years!"

Holy crap!

I needed to thoroughly inspect the aircraft log and maintenance records before even thinking about starting the engines, as I wondered what I had stumbled into. The information should have been made known upfront during initial negotiations. I had no one to blame but myself; that should have been the first question before any agreements were reached.

Excusing myself and stepping away, I called the mutual friend who had recommended me. "I have just found some disturbing information about this aircraft," I said. "Two years! It hadn't been flown in two years!" I screamed at him. "Would you know why it hadn't flown in two years, and why did you mention me to this guy?" I asked.

"Well, he is an old friend of mine in need of an experienced Hawker pilot, and knowing you were available, I thought you could use the work. I should have called you myself before recommending you. The Hawker he needs you to check out hasn't been flown for some time. I wasn't aware, however, that it had sat for two years.

"I had heard that the former owner/operator owed and reneged on thousands of dollars of maintenance, fuel, and storage fees. I don't know why Bimini was initially chosen as the maintenance facility for the Hawker back then.

Bimini wasn't an authorized Hawker repair shop. The former owner was from South America and had been shopping for a low-maintenance bid. He found one. Lots of that shit happens in South Florida. I heard the former owner lost it in a very contentious lawsuit. It had not flown since. Murphy had it painted and 're-ragged' to sell it. It had been advertised for sale for quite a while. It's hard to sell an old 600 without practically giving it away. It had been on his back ramp for over a year. I would advise you to look it over very carefully. I am sorry, bro. Just be careful!"

With that, the call ended, and so did our friendship.

Murphy opened the aircraft door while I was on the phone. He was joined by another person introduced to me as my co-pilot.

Before entering, I asked my new crew member how much experience he had in a Hawker jet. His sideways glance quickly shifted to Murphy, then back to me. "Zero, I fly a Learjet and have never flown a Hawker. How hard could it be?"

Confronted with a non-experienced co-pilot with a cavalier attitude and a devious contractual employer, I should have just walked away. Murphy apologized and said he would make it worth my while if I stuck around. I think he was reading my mind. Against my better judgment, I agreed to stick around if he agreed to a serious talk later. With that, I proceeded to get on with it.

When I entered the aircraft, I immediately turned left to the cockpit. There was a huge gaping hole in the center of the instrument panel.

Murphy said, "There had been an old-fashioned, outdated navigation computer that no longer worked, so I removed it."

I asked, "If the aircraft hadn't flown in two years, how did you know it was inoperative?"

"The former pilots told me," he said.

Curiouser and curiouser?

I was not familiar with any navigation computer that size installed in the 600-instrument panel or anywhere else in the cockpit, for that matter. It was a huge hole! I asked my questionable new co-pilot if he had ever seen what had been installed there.

"Hell, no. I have never even been in this aircraft until today."

Oh, my! What fun!

Perusing the aircraft log books a few days later, I discovered that the tail trim jack screw had been removed, serviced, and replaced. I could not find any write-up as to why it had been serviced. These maintenance logs were incomplete and suspicious. Checking with a couple of the maintenance techs, I was informed they had worked on the aircraft, but did not provide any more details about that particular write-up. At this point, I wasn't sure anything I found was authentic, which seriously troubled me.

Murphy was of little to no help, explaining that the log sheets were all he had regarding the past maintenance history. He mentioned, "The airplane flew here, so it was flyable then."

I said, "My concern is, is it flyable now?"

After three days of aircraft and Manit log inspections, I decided to start the engines for full-power engine runs. My co-pilot, Andy, tagged along to observe. The right engine refused to start. I asked Andy to step outside by the right engine to determine if he could hear the engine igniters clicking in an attempt to light the fire. After several attempts, he returned, saying he hadn't heard anything. I asked him to check the left side. I pushed the start button for the left engine, introduced fuel, and it started normally. I secured it and reported to Murphy, who sent two men to remove the right-hand igniter box. Two days later, we had a new box. The right engine started normally, and engine runs were successful.

I asked the control tower if we could perform a high-speed aborted takeoff on the runway during a lull in traffic. It was approved. I intended to check instruments, tires, and brakes. If I were expected to fly this thing, I wanted to stop it, if necessary, during the takeoff roll to confirm all instrumentation was working. I briefed Andy on the required callouts during the takeoff roll. I was most interested in "Airspeed Alive!" at a relatively slow speed when airflow would be introduced into the pitot tubes at around 60 knots. Power was applied, and we started accelerating.

Andy yelled: "Airspeed Alive."

I quickly checked my airspeed instrument. It stood at zero airspeed. I aborted. I had failed to tell Andy that he needed to cross-check BOTH airspeed instruments.

Back to the barn.

The tires looked okay at inspection, and the brake pads had been determined to have plenty left. They operated just fine. The 731 engines on this aircraft were not fitted with thrust reversers, which had been introduced in much newer Hawkers. The left pitot tubing was found to have a hornet's nest deep within it. It appeared to have been there a while.

After clearing the system, we tried another high-speed run down the runway. All seemed okay. The next thing was to muster the courage to take it into the air. I took a day off because it was the weekend. Murphy wasn't pleased, as he wanted everything to happen ASAP. I needed a day to get my courage up. Courage is being the only one who knows you're afraid. That was me because I didn't feel good about this machine.

Finally, the day arrived. I had spent several hours instructing and briefing Andy about my expectations. He was an experienced Learjet pilot, so I was confident he could land the thing if necessary. I filed a VFR flight plan as a round-robin test flight over the Atlantic. I intended to perform a few stalls at 17,500 ft and check all flight instruments and controls.

The tail jack screw service still nagged at me, so I made a mental note to go easy on the trim, its primary function.

On takeoff, I rolled a bit of nose-up trim as I rotated the

aircraft. We were straight out over the Atlantic, having taken off on the east runway.

Climbing out of about five thousand feet, I noticed that, even though I had been trimming the nose down, it was not responding. I pushed the elevators but could not lower my nose. The aircraft's attitude seemed fixed at about ten or twelve degrees nose up. I tried to re-trim it down, but couldn't. I then tried to trim it up to see if that would help get it unstuck, if that were the case. That was wrong! The nose rose a further 6 or 7 degrees, and it became challenging to control the damn thing. Andy and I pushed the elevator controls forward but could not get the nose down. Reducing power reduced the climb rate and speed. I had Andy declare an emergency as I sharply banked the airplane to return to FXE.

I noticed that the nose dropped in the heavily banked turn, but when I rolled out, the aircraft would return to a nose-high state again. Passing once again through five thousand feet in the turn, I decided that steep turns would, coupled with a judicious throttle movement, help control the altitude. I started a series of steep turns to lose altitude. Andy was talking to Approach Control, which had us on their radar. Explaining our erratic flight profile approach helped him to understand that this was the only way for us to control our descent. I am unsure how many 90-degree turns it took, but we finally had the runway in sight, at least while I rolled out of the turns for a look-see. I discovered that very steep turns on the final approach weren't a lot of fun.

Attempting to time the turns to roll out lined up with the runway with a nose-high attitude, I tried extending full flaps to see the effect. It initially dropped the nose somewhat, but then caused the nose to rise even higher while slowing the aircraft due to drag. I decided a no-flap landing would be better. I still had power, so speed wasn't an issue; I just had to get low enough in time to land. I didn't think that would be a problem. I managed to get the aircraft pretty low as we continually crossed the runway's center line. At somewhere around 50 ft, I rolled out nose high on the center line, pulled the power off, landed on the stall stick-shaker, and, in a slight right bank, bounced once and stopped. What an exercise! Later, I got shit-faced!

It was determined that the incorrect grease had been used on the jack screw, causing it to freeze up and jam. That and the fact it hadn't been used in two years contributed to this mishap. The local FAA guys showed up and wanted a report from me. They demanded to see all the aircraft's records, flight, and maintenance.

Netjets, the large quarter-share operator based at the main Fort Lauderdale Airport, operated several newer Hawker 1000 jets. Exceptionally familiar with the type, the FAA requested them to come to FXE, examine the aircraft, and then report their findings. Murphy was in trouble. I had written and submitted my report and bid Mr. Murphy "Adieu."

Chapter Ten
"LISTEN UP!"

Gulliver's Travels!

As one aspires to become a pilot, serious study, practice, and financial assistance are often required. The goal, of course, is the coveted private pilot's license. If one desires to fly for a living, requirements increase, as do the workload and study involved. The goal for many is the coveted airline job. Usually, this will happen only when a few benchmarks have been achieved: a commercial pilot's license, an instrument rating, and a multi-engine endorsement, as well as several hundred flight hours generally accrued as a certified flight instructor. Attached to all of that are the hopes and dreams of a career that only a few are able to accomplish.

As flying hours and experience are gained, other facets of aviation may become equally desirable, such as military, corporate, or charter aviation. Military aviation particularly has enjoyed a recent resurgence with the popularity of Top Gun, Maverick. Corporate, charter, and airline aviation are finding it difficult to recruit suitably experienced pilots. Airlines have had trouble filling cockpits vacated by seasoned pilots taking early retirement.

A few airlines, such as United, have established their flight schools to train student pilots from scratch, gradually advancing them to the right seat of their regional carriers and eventually to the cockpit of a major airline. There is a pilot shortage, the blame for which can be squarely placed at the feet of the COVID-19 pandemic. The pandemic has eased, but the shortage lingers.

Long before the aberration called COVID, and as previously mentioned a few chapters ago, my career began as a 'Freight Dog' in the right seat of a WWII aircraft lovingly referred to as 'Dumbo'—the venerable C-46 Curtis Commando. Eventually, I qualified as a captain. One day, I had an opportunity to interview with Allegheny Airlines, later known as USAir. I interviewed and was ultimately hired by Captain Harvey Gulf, one of the airline's recruiters. I soon found myself in the right seat of a French Nord 232 aircraft. It didn't take long before boredom set in. Flying between the same cities, day after day, proved monotonous and commonplace.

Less challenging as days wore on, soon the dread of each day bore heavily; the weight slowly became unbearable. After a time, I resigned prematurely, some say, as the promise of flying larger aircraft with different route structures was promised.

It has often been said that "flying for a living was always better than working for a living." That colloquial expression, I found, was only accurate when I discovered corporate aviation. After several false starts and disappointments with a few unscrupulous operators, such as the one in Ft. Lauderdale, my spirit, far from broken, finally paid off. I became Midwest's newest pilot of a large corporate flight department. Transporting company executives to many cities domestically and internationally was challenging and exciting. While difficult, the advantages of the corporate pilot are often beyond all other endeavors in airborne transportation. Traveling the world and visiting exotic locations for days and frequently weeks with all expenses paid are beyond what could have been imagined. While airline flying can often be quite lucrative, it simply can't compare to a week or two of paid vacation in a luxurious resort in a fabled location. That is not to say that corporate pilots don't earn their keep.

Crew training requirements and certifications were as stringent as I discovered at the airline. During my limited airline flying experience, I found that practically everything except flying the plane and the preflight inspection was accomplished by other people.

As we passed through operations on a flight day, weather updates, fuel requirements, weight and balance info, and passenger count were handed to us as a packet. Airline flight crews have little, if any, interaction with their passengers. The opposite is true of corporate crews. Pilots were now expected and required to perform all the above and several additional tasks, such as catering, filing flight plans, acquiring car rentals, limo bookings, and crew accommodations. Route and destination weather forecasts were just a few of the many tasks required to commence and complete a successful flight.

My new company was a multinational corporation. The flight department consisted of three sizable corporate jet aircraft and twelve pilots. I had been warned that the board's chairman was a no-nonsense, brilliant, and determined individual who often exhibited a short fuse when his plans seemed awry. "He could be scatterbrained about simple daily things most of us take for granted. Beware!" I was warned.

Absorbed in the daily workings of the company, the chairman left many of the finer details of his impending trips on the corporate aircraft to others. Secretaries and Girl Fridays were employed to type itineraries, select and book hotels, and arrange ground transportation at destination cities, often ordering specified catering to be delivered to the aircraft. After close consultation with the chairman, his staff provided these details to the flight crews.

Problems would sometimes arise when the chairman's thoughts were not communicated, or the notetakers omitted his thoughts. Unfortunately, the latter was usually singled out as the sole factor when these events occurred, and this became almost commonplace. Several episodes come to mind.

While on a very short final approach to Rwy 25L at LAX, suddenly, the chairman ran up to the cockpit: "Where are we? Shit, this is Los Angeles; PULL UP! Shit, I told them I needed to go to Santa Ana. PULL UP!"

"Too late! We are committed," I replied. (We were descending through 200 ft for landing at the time). "Sit down and strap in."

We could have gone around, but ATC would not have cheerfully welcomed that decision. We landed and then refiled a flight plan for SNA. The chairman blamed and unloaded on the crew for this miscommunication, then phoned the home office and unloaded on them. The previous warnings were exemplified; this would not be my last encounter with that short fuse.

He enjoyed a lovely home in an exclusive gated community in Manalapan, Fla. En route to Fort Lauderdale from the Indiana home office, one evening, he appeared cheerful. He was looking forward to a few days of R&R. As we descended into the FLL area, he entered the cockpit and said, "Where are we?"

From past experiences, that soon-to-become familiar question put us both on alert. "Descending into Ft. Lauderdale," I responded.

"Dammit, I told you I needed to land at Palm Beach. My wife is meeting me there! We are driving to FLL! Shit," he yelled.

"You might have told someone, boss, but not us. It's no problem; we can still land at PBI since we haven't passed it yet," I said.

While this exchange occurred, my co-pilot immediately informed ATC of a destination change, defusing the situation. It didn't take long before I realized I needed to confirm his itinerary as soon as he boarded the aircraft.

Another of the more memorable events had nothing to do with his itinerary. A substantial and essential business venture initiated and funded by our company in San Antonio, Texas, was soon to have its grand opening. The company was to be represented by several executives and the chairman. The chairman was to fly solo on his primary aircraft, and the execs followed in another aircraft. I was once again selected to fly the chairman that day.

Arriving at the airport dressed in jeans and carrying his hang-up bag, he said, "Let me know when we are thirty minutes from landing."

Receiving his thirty-minute warning, he changed into his formal attire. We had been informed that Texas Governor Mark White, the mayor of San Antonio, Henry Cisneros, and all the TV affiliate stations were to be awaiting our arrival. Arriving on the corporate aircraft ramp, we were surprised to see several hundred folks smiling and waving.

Cameras flashed, and TV cameramen aimed their cameras as they followed the aircraft to our parking stand. It was a windy day, and the TV guys appeared hard put to hold their cameras steady while a few ladies clutched at their skirts.

Engines secured and wheels choked, I opened the door. The boss was standing to the side, hidden from the reception. Standing beside and out of sight, next to the air stair opening, I noticed his fly was open. "Boss! Your fly is open," I called as the stairs descended.

His white shirt tail slightly protruded from the opening, appearing as a white flag waving in the wind. He either didn't hear me or chose to ignore me. I could see he was about to step into the limelight. Slightly panicking, I attempted emphatically again, this time louder and more emphatic: "Boss, your fly is open," I all but yelled.

Too late, he stepped into the doorway, waving his arms, smiling as the TV cameras followed him down the air stairs. Following subtly behind him as he descended the steps, I gently touched his arm to warn him that he was waving more than his arms. The governor and the mayor stepped forward with welcoming smiles, shaking hands. I tried to get his attention by whispering to him and slightly touching his arm once again. Becoming agitated and aggravated by this persistent pilot at his side, he momentarily forgot where he was. Turning toward me, he said loudly and emphatically, "What the hell do you want?"

"Your fly is open!" I whispered, attempting to offer him as dignified an opportunity as possible to turn away from the crowd and address the problem.

Nope! Instead, he repeated louder than I had hoped, ***"My Fly is open!"***

The declaration was announced to all who hadn't yet noticed but now became aware, causing quite a bit of laughter and not a little embarrassment as he giggled and turned away from the cameras to close the offending hatch. At least I tried.

The evening news captured the entire event with comments such as: "There were two openings taking place in San Antonio today," and, from the weatherman, "The First 'White flag' San Antonio has ever seen on its soil," referring to the Alamo's refusal to surrender.

In retrospect, it was pretty darn funny. The boss passed away a couple of years ago. Arriving at the Pearly Gates and looking around, I'll just bet he asked St. Peter, "Where are we?"

Chapter Eleven
"A DARK AND STORMY NIGHT"

An older Hawker jet 400A model

Ask any pilot what he thinks of New York's LaGuardia Airport, and they will no doubt say: "Not Much." With its short runways, congested ramps, taxiways, and inimical tower controllers, you have a recipe for frustration, stress, and angst.

"Hawker 61MS; LaGuardia Ground: Be advised you're number 31 for takeoff."

Asking if we could move the aircraft off the Marine Air Terminal General Aviation Ramp, we were told to join taxiway 'B' (Bravo) to taxiway 'F' (Foxtrot), right turn on taxiway 'F' to hold short of taxiway 'BB.' (Bravo-Bravo)

Reading back about the clearance, we advised that we would be securing engines. Still, we would have the APU (Auxiliary Power Unit) online to monitor ground control and tower frequency.

Departures were sporadic as the wind blew at 20+ knots, gusting to 30+ knots, and seldom down the runway. As a result, the crosswind was often beyond what was allowable for most aircraft. We were at the mercy of the wind as it violently shook the aircraft. Controls were locked as they were being knocked about to prevent them from being damaged.

The company CEO was our only passenger and the world's most impatient traveler. When we explained our delay, he badgered us to get moving. Explaining the nature of the delay left him unhappy and grumbling to himself. He eventually settled down and accepted his fate. About 20 minutes into our wait, ground control announced that a weather frontal passage was about to occur.

"Everyone listen up," said ground control. "Folks, we are changing runway operations due to frontal passage. Who's #1 for runway 31?"

"USAir 21 is #1 for 31."

"USAir 21 taxi onto Rwy 31, and exit at taxiway Yankee to Oscar to Rwy 4. Who's #2?"

"Piedmont 630 is #2."

"Piedmont, follow USAir. Who's #3?

"TWA 12 is #3."

"TWA follow behind Piedmont. Everyone waiting at Rwy 31, follow the chain to Rwy 4."

Shortly after the ground controller spoke his last remark, we heard: "Ground, Piedmont 630."

"Go ahead, Piedmont, this is Ground."

"Roger Ground, we just joined taxiway Oscar at Foxtrot and took a hit from an errant TWA baggage cart near the left wing. We're shutting down engines...." (The baggage cart had broken loose from a tug and was propelled by the wind into the side of the aircraft.)

In a high-pitched and excited voice, ground control responded: *"SAY AGAIN PIEDMONT???"*

Piedmont repeated his last transmission.

"Oh BOY, OH BOY! EVERYBODY STOP!" yelled the ground controller.

"Ground One, are you on frequency?" (Referring to the airport ground vehicle.)

In a very typical New York accent, ground one answered the controller: "Err ah yeah der ground, dis is ground one. Go ahead." (Think Archie Bunker)

"Ground One, Ground, I need you to proceed to taxiway Oscar and Foxtrot at the tower's base. A Piedmont 737 claims he was struck by a TWA baggage cart and report back."

"Err, ah, Roger, okay der ground. Ground One."

After several minutes, we heard: "Err, ah, Ground, dis is Ground One."

"Go ahead, Ground One, Ground."

"Err, ah, Ground; It appears da Perpetrator, Penetrated da Piedmont Airliner at da left-wing root adjourning da fuse ledge."

Then, another voice from an unknown airliner: "Is it still red?"

Still another: "Penetration, however slight." (Quoting the legal definition of rape!)

At this point, the ground controller was ready to fall on his sword. "Everybody shut up, don't talk!" he screamed.

We were cracking up in the cockpit, hearing this exchange. You can't imagine what a monumental operation this was. Thirty-plus aircraft were waiting for their turn to take off, and many were still waiting at the gate. Eventually, the baggage cart was carefully removed from the side of the aircraft. The aircraft was towed onto a vacant ramp as no gates were available to offload the passengers. During this operation, a biblical rain event began as buses were dispatched to retrieve some miserable and wet passengers back to the terminal.

We finally reached our lucky number for take-off and departed, laughing all the way back to home base. And my F/O, I in the cockpit that night, still cracks up all these years later, remembering the events of that evening and ole Archie Bunker manning the airport ground vehicle. He was Archie before Archie!

Today, LaGuardia Airport's beautiful passenger terminals have been completely renovated. However, the ramps and runways remain as congested as they always were.

Chapter Twelve
"WHAT THE HELL WAS THAT?"

We had been in Las Vegas for two days and were bored. My co-pilot and I suffered a few gambling losses at the Tropicana, so we decided to drive around town. Passing Caesars Palace, my F/O claimed he had never been to Caesars. Turning around, we pulled up at the concierge parking stand. Once inside, I decided to try my luck one more time at the crap tables. A rather large and boisterous crowd had gathered around one table. Investigating, it seemed someone was having a great run. Attempting to nudge my way through the crowd to get closer, a hand grabbed my shoulder and spun me around rather abruptly. It was one of the owners of the company.

"Eddie, take this and give it to me tomorrow night when we depart LAS."

He drunkenly handed me a thick manila envelope and added, "Guard it with your life!"

I stuffed it into my pocket, which took some doing as it was pretty thick.

The shouting, it seems, was in support of his brother, who was rolling the dice. He had made his fifth straight pass, collecting a bundle each time. Some people have all the luck. It takes money to make money, and they had plenty.

Soon, bored watching multi-millionaires become wealthier, we left the casino as I lost more money, again at the tables. Our rental car had been left in valet parking. While waiting for the valet, I reached into my pocket. There was the envelope. I had almost forgotten about it. Tipping the valet, I climbed behind the wheel, depositing the envelope in the glove compartment. The next day, we drove to Lake Mead and Hoover Dam. The casinos were becoming tiring, and there were only so many times one could watch the 'Dancing Waters' at the Bellagio. Scheduled for a 9 pm departure and unable to take in a show or drink, this would be a long day.

Arriving at McCarron Field at eight that night, we set about getting the aircraft ready with catering, filing a flight plan, and checking the Met reports for our flight route. We also checked Notams for our departure and landing airports. Long ago, I learned a severe lesson about checking NOTAMs for departure and arrival fields.

I was familiar with the owner's brother's propensity to be very late for departure, having been employed by them for over 12 years at this point in my career. They didn't disappoint! They showed up at midnight, drunk and staggering as they boarded the aircraft with four other company executives. (Later, they would no longer fly together on the same plane.)

The takeoff was uneventful. Climbing to FL370 (thirty-seven thousand feet), the autopilot was switched on as we settled for a smooth flight. About twenty minutes later, and with a fresh cup of hot coffee in my hand, there was a tremendous BANG from what seemed like outside and directly over the cockpit. The second bang was my heart as adrenaline hit. The hot coffee hit my lap. Noticing my co-pilot had instantly gotten his oxygen mask on and was breathing heavily, I first thought we had a midair collision with something or someone. The board's chairman stumbled to the cockpit, white as the proverbial ghost, screaming and demanding, "What the hell was that?"Pointing to my F/O: "Why is he wearing a mask? What's that light?"

The #2 low-pressure fuel light had illuminated. I emphatically told him to sit down and strap in. Returning to the cabin, he screamed in a drunken slur, "Everyone, get your masks on!"

This, of course, caused even more panic among the drunks. I yelled that that was unnecessary and asked everyone to stay seated with their seat belts on. Of course, the masks were still stowed, deploying only if the cabin lost pressure, which it did not.

We were still pressurized. Thank God for small favors!

The banging had now moved to the aircraft's rear with no definite cadence and was intermittent. Engine instruments were all normal, but that #2 fuel low-pressure light was illuminated on the annunciator panel. WTF?

Reducing power on both engines seemed to mitigate the banging as the aircraft slowed. Once again, applying power on one engine at a time seemed to have no appreciable effect. We advised Albuquerque Center that we had a "slight" problem and wished to land immediately at Flagstaff, AZ, just off our right wing.

The chairman's brother picked this time to ask me for the manila envelope. He bragged that it contained 'a lot of money.' If they were going to die, he wanted the money. Oh Shit! I had forgotten about it. It had been left in the glove compartment of the Hertz rental as if I didn't have enough problems. A possible midair, a damaged aircraft, an airplane full of panicking drunks, and missing what I suspected were some big bucks. My whole life flashed in front of me. I was sure that events were proving to be resume-producing.

Focusing on the continuous and intermittent banging and the low-pressure fuel light, I was out of solutions. Could the single-point fueling cap have been left off and dangling in the slipstream? No, that couldn't be it, as the problem would have manifested sooner.

Besides, my co-pilot, who was becoming lightheaded from breathing pure oxygen, rapidly fueling his angst, swore he did a preflight walk-around, and all was good.

What the hell was it? What could it be?

It is a bit trite, as I have said it before, "You fly an aircraft with your head, not your hands."

I kept looking around in hopes of seeing something I missed. I was familiar with this aircraft, having flown it over six thousand hours at the time, but NADA!

Descending slowly from altitude in case of structural damage, the banging also seemed to slow. We were talking to Albuquerque Center. The controller kept asking: "Hawker 62MS, is everything okay?"

"Yes, sir. Just a minor problem," I lied.

That damned light was making me angry. The #2 engine was running fine despite the low-pressure light, but I selected fuel cross-feed just in case. Entering the Flagstaff pattern, the tower cleared us to land. I was unsure if selecting landing flaps would present a problem, so I decided on a partial flap landing. The banging was nonexistent; however, the low-pressure fuel light remained on.

As we taxied onto the well-lit ramp, two people, I assumed to be pilots, waited as we passed; both pointed to the rear of the aircraft. *That can't be good!* After securing the engines, I had to fight the chairman for the door handle.

He wanted out ASAP and didn't know how to open it, but it made no difference. He was so excited by fear and adrenaline that he might have gotten it open, albeit with bloody hands as he clawed at it! It's incredible what panic will do to some folks.

I was first out, and seeing nothing immediately, I ran to the other side. Sighting down the side of the aircraft and looking at the single-point fueling area, all was well until I looked up. There, loosely hanging, was the HF antenna, attached to the early Hawker aircraft above the cockpit, stretched and then fastened to the tail. As it explosively detached itself from above the cockpit, it wrapped itself around the aircraft's tail with the large attachment 'ball' of some serious hard epoxy smashing intermittently into the tail. I was later told that aerodynamically, that was impossible. *Yeah, uh-huh! Who'd a thunk it? But that damn fuel light?*

Climbing back aboard, I fired up the APU. Both fuel switches were selected, but #2 still indicated inoperative. Hmm! Some of you pilots reading this may have guessed by now that, in the heat of the emergency, given that the light came on almost simultaneously, I never thought to check the bloody circuit breaker on the breaker panel just behind the F/O's head. When my co-pilot snapped his mask from the hook behind his head so quickly, he inadvertently pulled out the #2 fuel low-pressure breaker simultaneously. Lesson learned!

There is an old saying: "Good judgment comes from experience, and experience comes from bad judgment!"

SLOW DOWN and THINK!

Then, I was once again asked for the money. Terrified that it was gone, I asked him to stand by. I rushed inside to make a call to Hertz Vegas. (There were no cell phones in those days.) Thank goodness they never close in Vegas. After explaining my problem, I reached a young lady who said it had been found. She explained that it had been opened but not counted and had been resealed. "Give me an address, and we will expedite and insure it for you."

I fessed up and was called several names I won't mention here. Many threats later, we departed again after cutting the line from the tail. The next day, the package arrived, having been placed with an airline crew for a counter-to-counter delivery. (Before the days of FedEx and UPS, you could expedite a small package for a fee that would be handed to the flight crew for delivery to the airline's ticket counter at the destination. Thus, 'Counter to Counter.')

Thankfully, it was all there, thank God. Of course, I had my ass chewed out royally, but because they all thought I saved their life, I received a nice bonus coupled with a threat of unemployment with another careless slip-up. Ya, Mun!

Another day in the life!

Chapter Thirteen
"MICROBURST[1]"

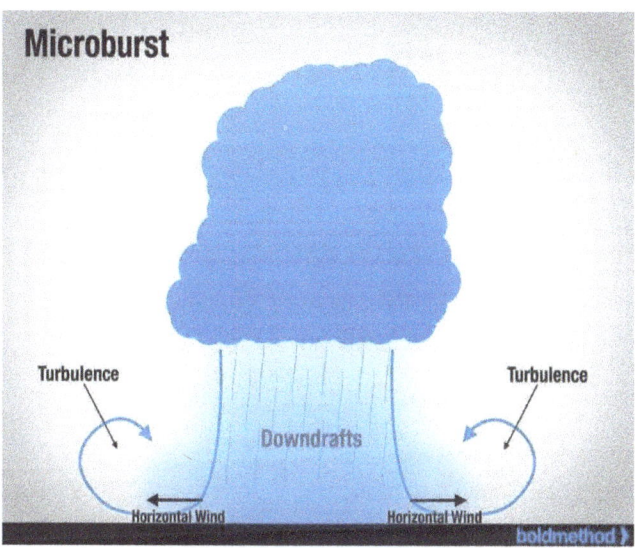

Microburst

Turbulence

Turbulence

Downdrafts

Horizontal Wind

Horizontal Wind

boldmethod ⟩

T he Hawker 700 model was a bit underpowered for a midsize corporate jet. I had several thousand hours of experience in the model and was used to its shortcomings. My F/O on this particular flight was also aware of and very experienced in the aircraft.

We had left Aspen, CO, a couple of hours before and were to land at Palwaukee Airport (now Chicago Executive Airport) in Wheeling, Illinois. It was raining heavily and approaching thunderstorms with gusty winds.

It would be nighttime upon our arrival.

---

[1] *mi·cro·burst/ˈmī-krō-ˌbərst Violent short-lived localized downdraft that creates extreme wind shears at low altitudes and is usually associated with thunderstorms.*

Commencing from the west and being radar-vectored around and through a weather front, more than a few active thunderstorms flashed and crashed in their relentless march eastward. Our airborne cockpit radar was bathed in RED in every quadrant, lending credibility to the folly of our arrogance. Descending through the turbulence and heavy rain, deviating as much as we dared while being vectored by the Chicago ARTC (Air Route Traffic Control) was becoming problematic as aircraft were holding or being held all around us as the extremely busy aircraft controller kept us clear to the north of Chicago's O'Hare Airport and the now saturated holding airspace. (O'Hare lies just 10 miles south of the Palwaukee Airport).

Handed off to the final approach controller, we threaded the needle in what appeared to be a Herculean effort of the true professional aircraft controller. My responsibility was to keep my four passengers safe, while the controllers were to keep thousands of passengers safe. I don't know how they do it.

Controller burnout is severe, especially on high-volume, extreme weather days like this. The approach was commenced using autopilot as the turbulence was severe and problematic. The instrument approach was to Rwy16 at PWK. The winds were reported to be from 240 degrees to 280 degrees at a steady 15 knots, with gusts to 25 to 30 knots and peak gusts to 42.

The ceiling was reported as ragged at 400' to 600', with forecasted ceilings to drop below landing minimums of 200' within the next hour.

Disengaging the autopilot at two hundred feet and struggling to correct for the wind, the touchdown was smooth due to the wet 75' wide runway. (Rwy 16/34 has since been widened to 150'.) The gusty winds made good use of the rudder pedals during the landing rollout to keep the aircraft on the runway's center line.

The plane attempted to hydroplane momentarily during deceleration but was quickly brought under control. We planned to drop our passengers and immediately depart for Indianapolis, IN, our home base. The term used was 'One Engine Turn or Quick Turn.'

Only one engine would be shut down to facilitate deplaning the passengers as quickly as possible, thus spending as little time on the ground as possible. The secured engine would be restarted on taxi-out while checklists were completed and airway clearances were received.

Upon reaching the departure end of Rwy 34, which was now in use due to the variable winds, I activated the airborne weather radar on the ground, overriding the WOW switch (Weight-on-Wheels), which kills the airborne radar on touchdown. Facing west, the radar screen had once again shown red while painting (radar depiction) the thunder cells that, while closer to us now, were still several miles to the west.

The winds buffeted the aircraft as I moved the plane in a semicircle to get a definitive radar read on the extent of the storms. Satisfied that there weren't any thunderstorms immediately overhead, we requested and received takeoff clearance.

The aircraft accelerated to rotate speed rather quickly. Pulling back on the controls to become airborne, the nose lifted off, but the main gear remained planted firmly on the runway. Working the rudder pedals to keep the aircraft on the runway while pulling further back on the controls appeared ineffective as copious amounts of the available runway were being devoured. My F/O, also pulling on the controls, yelled that the end of the runway was rapidly approaching. As the last few feet of runway passed below the nose of the aircraft, the main gear suddenly left the ground, launching the plane with an attitude of over 30 degrees nose up, instantly activating the Stall Warning (Stick Shaker).

The total amount of back pressure applied to become airborne now needed immediate reversing to lower the nose. My attention was on the dangerously and rapidly disappearing airspeed. Experiencing an incredible tailwind, the aircraft was no longer in the grips of the downburst but was now caught in the outflow as it spread across the ground in all directions. Leveling the plane at less than 100 ft, the speed slowly increased, intermittently silencing the 'stick shaker' as control was slowly and fully restored. Still tuned to the tower frequency, the tower called and asked if we had experienced any difficulty.

They indicated they had indications of a possible Microburst over the field during our takeoff roll. Yup, you might say that! The aircraft had been pinned to the ground, unable to become airborne until we miraculously traveled out of its clutches. On becoming airborne, the tailwind we experienced almost brought the aircraft down until we could regain speed and control. God had quite literally been our co-pilot that night.

Several takeaways from this experience:

- You don't need an active thunderstorm overhead to produce violent winds and a microburst.
- Never overlook that you are human and are often prone to believe you are better and more skilled than you might be.
- If it looks that bad, it probably is. Stay on the ground!

When I started my flying career several years ago, I started with a bag full of luck and an empty bag of experience. I was fortunate enough to fill the bag of experience before I emptied the bag of luck.

Chapter Fourteen
"HEAT OF THE MOMENT"

S hortly after I started flying the Hawker jet, I received a call that a friend of mine had been involved in a severe incident in a Hawker in California. This is what happened to my friend.

Every field of endeavour has its limitations in one form or another. 'Limitations' are not merely interesting reading; if exceeded, failures in one form or another, possibly approaching catastrophic, could occur. In several instances, rules have been ignored, often resulting in the complete loss of the aircraft and life. Here is an example of an aircraft loss that occurred because the rules were disregarded. Published for the initiated and uninitiated alike, they aim to evoke an interest beyond casual, mandating adherence and establishing a safety line that must never be crossed. Whether a new aspirant or an experienced pilot, they serve as unimpeachable 'rules-of-the-road.'

Several years ago, an advertisement appeared for a Type Rated Hawker 800 pilot for a short-term domestic contract flying. This was a co-pilot/first officer position. It failed to mention that it would assist a newly type-rated Hawker captain. Contract flying can often be lucrative, sometimes gratifying, and always interesting. Flying with a previously unknown pilot can be fun or your worst nightmare. This contract proved to be the latter, and for an unsuspecting professional, it almost ruined his career.

This day, the weather was clear at SNA (Santa Anna, CA), and there was a mild wind from the west. The Hawker jet was due to depart for the home base on a deadhead flight. (No Pax) Engines were started, checklists completed, and take-off clearance was requested and granted. The aircraft was lightweight, with only the minimum fuel required for the trip and the mandatory reserve fuel amount.

As power was added, the aircraft accelerated rapidly toward its take-off speed. Suddenly and without warning, the captain yelled, "Abort!"

Retarding the throttles, deploying the thrust reversers, and selecting lift dump, which extended the flaps to approximately seventy degrees, providing maximum drag in slowing the aircraft. The F/O was surprised as he had been monitoring the engine instruments. All seemed normal.

Clearing the runway at the end, the co-pilot (my friend) asked, "Why did you abort?"

A mumbled response came to the effect "It didn't feel right."

The F/O said everything looked good engine-wise. "What did you feel?"

His response again was "It just didn't feel right." He said, "Let's do a power check, and if it's okay, we will try it again."

As an experienced Hawker captain, the F/O mentioned that the last speed he saw as the abort was called was just below 90 knots and that a wait of 25 minutes was mandatory per op specs and limitations. Limitations for the Hawker 800 say that for an abort below 90 knots, a compulsory wait of 25 minutes must be followed; if a second abort is made below 90 knots, a mandatory wait of 45 minutes must be followed. A mandatory brake inspection must be made if an abort exceeds 90 knots.

The power check was normal. The captain then requested take-off clearance. The F/O spoke up, saying it hadn't been twenty-five minutes since the last abort. He was ignored as the tower cleared the Hawker for another go. Throttles were briskly advanced as the aircraft accelerated rapidly. "ABORT!" was yelled yet again at just below 90 knots.

Maximum braking was applied. The aircraft deceleration was markedly reduced due to the still-hot braking from the first abort.

It proceeded slightly onto the overrun portion of the runway. Incredulous, the F/O asked again what was happening as everything seemed normal. The captain again said, "It just didn't feel right."

"Per the limitations, we must wait at least 45 minutes before we can try this again, but I think we should cancel and have someone check the aircraft," said the F/O.

The tower operator had been watching their progress. Noticing smoke and flames erupting from the left main gear as the aircraft cleared the runway, he immediately signalled an aircraft fire emergency, alerting fire equipment and crew. The brakes were extremely hot, burning through the brake hydraulic line, catching fire immediately. The crew hurriedly deplaned as the aircraft burned.

When the emergency fire equipment arrived, the fire was raging and about to reach the wing tanks. Thankfully, it was rapidly extinguished, and there was no explosion. There were no fatalities except for the aircraft.

The Hawker 800 aircraft has a belly fuel tank called the 'Ventral' tank. Had it been fueled (it must be fueled fully), the Hawker may have exploded with two fatalities aboard. The FAA suspended both pilots' certificates for six months. The successful completion of an FAA 709 flight check was required to reinstate their respective licenses at the end of that period.

(A 'Do or Die' Check ride, if failed, your certificate is permanently revoked.) Both pilots were without a paycheck during this period. The F/O paid for his retraining to ensure he passed the 709 check.

He did. It is not known if the captain passed his 709 check. Retraining was called for in his case, with a strong emphasis on 'Limitations!'

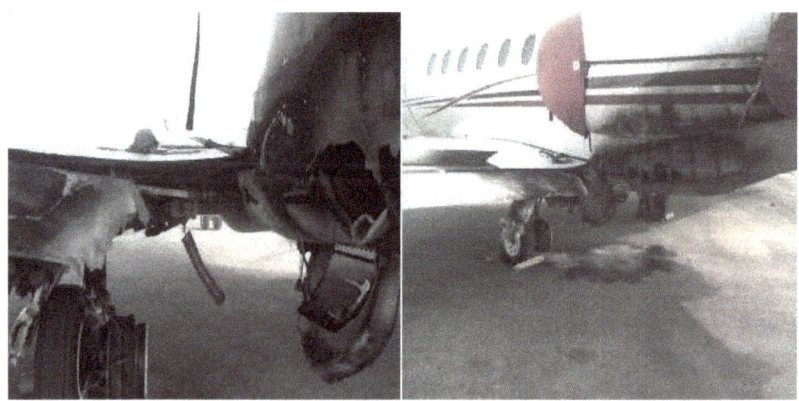

Aftermath of that Limitation Violation

Chapter Fifteen
"ASPEN, TESTING THE LIMITS!"

Approach to Aspen Airport

An Appreciation Event!

This event had me fighting for control, as in a previous chapter, due to someone else's lapse in judgment. (Some lessons take a while to sink in.)The aircraft was the same Hawker 700 I was very familiar with. Unfortunately, I had grown overly confident and complacent with my abilities and experience in this model. A 'deadly combination.'

Aspen, Colo., rests in the gentle and majestic Roaring Fork Valley, providing majestic backdrops for the senses. Snuggled among the foothills and lying at the base of mountains such as Aspen Mountain, commonly called Ajax and Snowmass, is the Aspen/Pitkin County Airport—just 'ASPEN' in pilot speak. The airport lies at 7815 ft MSL. The runway had been extended from 6,000 ft to 7,006 ft in 1983 and, in 2011, to its current length of 8,006 ft.

All pilots planning a trip to Aspen should do so cautiously and have a thorough understanding of the requisites of mountain flying. Aspen winter weather lends itself wonderfully to the skiing enthusiast while presenting many challenges for the pilots. Summer temperatures, usually with low humidity, are equally challenging as warmer temperatures degrade aircraft performance. It is expected to see density altitudes in excess of 10,000 ft as early as 10 am on summer mornings. Understanding density altitude and its effect on aircraft performance is a requisite.

In the late '70s, as a new captain for a large Midwestern corporation that operated three Hawker jet aircraft, two model 700s and an older Viper-powered 400 model, I flew many trips to Aspen during the winter and summer. Initially, my experience flying there was limited, but I soon became more confident, proficient, and accepting of the fickle mountainous weather proclivities. Mentored earlier by a well-experienced and older Aspen/mountain pilot, I was his ardent student.

Recognizing a new propensity on my part to be a bit casual when talking about a few past Aspen trips, he warned me, "Aspen is like a female praying mantis. It will give birth to your joy of being there one minute and, the next, devour you! Hopefully, you will be smart enough to avoid what I call an 'Aspen Appreciation Event.' If you are foolish enough to encounter one of your own doing or survive, you will understand my meaning."

(Aspen Appreciation Event = a dangerously close call involving an approach or departure from Aspen/Pitkin County Airport, thus giving an appreciation of the inherent and unforgiving dangers of possible faulty decision-making).

I laughed it off at the time.

Arriving in Aspen at 9 am with six company executives for a long-awaited seminar in the heart of the Rockies, we were greeted with a beautiful summer mountain morning. A rippling air of excitement and anticipation, fueled by the smell of clear mountain air and beautiful Aspens framed against towering mountain vistas, greeted them as they stepped from the aircraft. Among the passengers was a lovely young woman with a gorgeous smile that would have made the devil whimper. Unbeknownst to me at the time, I would later be similarly affected.

Only a few hours of their day were dedicated to the seminar. Much of the time was spent touring, hiking, and enjoying the grand restaurants and happy hour offerings.

Soon, three days passed, and our day of departure arrived.

It was another magnificent summer day. I was scheduled to depart at 10 am before the cooler morning air gave way to afternoon heat, so density altitude concerns were foremost in my mind. Unfortunately, the departure time passed as temperatures steadily rose in concert with my concerns. At 1 pm, it was 83 degrees Fahrenheit and rising. Repeated attempts to reach the group proved unsuccessful. They finally arrived at 1:30 pm, and an additional passenger, a rather large man, was added to the group of six. I did not need a chance encounter with an old friend who needed a ride, accompanied by his excessive baggage. "We didn't think you would mind, Captain."

I did mind with ever-mounting trepidation.

I had planned a technical stop at Pueblo, Colorado, and had fueled accordingly for the now missed 10 am departure. That would have presented an uneventful take-off. Now, however, things were not at all favourable for aircraft performance. I confronted the lead passenger with my concerns. "It would be best to wait for the temperature to cool before we attempt a takeoff," I said.

He seemed considerate of my suggestion, but... (It should have been a demand, not a suggestion. Retrospect has a way of clearing one's vision, albeit a bit late.) The woman with the unbelievably attractive smile, overhearing the conversation, interrupted and asked if there was any way we could depart. She mentioned earlier receiving a call from her mother regarding her son's very high temperature. There was that smile again.

On its best day, the Hawker 700 was slightly underpowered for a summertime afternoon takeoff from Aspen. Consulting the QRH (Quick Reference Handbook), the takeoff numbers barely appeared in the high-shaded area. (Shaded area numbers were best avoided as they indicated degraded aircraft performance.) This brought to mind Dirty Harry when he said, "Do you feel lucky, punk?"

We had numbers; it's just that they indicated a somewhat nebulous aircraft performance. I decided to go. Was it a decision to please that smile? Perhaps.

As we taxied out to Rwy 33, I was glad it had a 2% downhill slope that might help ever so slightly with acceleration. Cleared for take-off, I applied full static power and released the brakes. The aircraft slowly started rolling. I felt the rolling was more because of the 2% downhill slope than the power application.

The usual visual cue I used to judge the takeoff performance at Aspen was passing the FBO (Fixed Base Operation) building, a little over halfway down the runway, at 100 knots or more. This time, we passed the building at slightly above 80 knots and accelerated much slower than usual.

"End coming up!" Rick, my F/O, yelled.

Not quite yet at the rotation speed, I had no choice but to rotate the aircraft as I felt the main gear slipping off the end of the runway."Gear up!" I yelled as we barely cleared the fence at the far end of the runway.

The stick shaker (stall warning) was constant. Just across Rt. 82, the highway just beyond the departure end of the runway, there was a depression in the terrain, Woody Creek. Gently lowering the nose slightly into that depression, the speed slowly increased. The stick shaker now only intermittently tickled the yoke until we slowly climbed out of that hole. In a concerned voice, the tower asked if we were experiencing a problem. We did not reply. Eventually, after seeing us climb slowly out of Woody Creek, the controller advised us rather breathlessly to contact departure.

Hawker's main bleed air valves provide pressurization and are usually turned on right after takeoff. When on, they slightly steal power from the engines to supply the air needed for pressurization. We held the valves and our breath. Passing through approximately 12,000 ft, we heard a commotion from the back. In those anxious moments right after that adrenaline-filled departure, we had overlooked turning on the air valves and were not pressurizing; thus, the oxygen masks, set to deploy when cabin altitude reached 12,300 ft, caused quite a stir. The 'rubber jungle' surprised and terrified some passengers who donned the masks immediately. The air valves were immediately switched on. We were now pressurizing as the air entered the cabin with a vengeance, attempting to 'cone head' everyone.

After blaming sticky air valves and apologizing, I explained that they would have to deal with the dangling masks until arriving at Pueblo, where we would attempt to re-stow them.

Upon landing at Pueblo, that enchanting smile approached to thank me for my consideration, as she felt I departed only because she had asked. She wasn't too far from wrong. "You were very courageous!" she said.

I thought, *"Courage is being the only one who knows you are scared." After the fact, I certainly was.*

It took until landing at PUB for my hands to stop shaking. It was quite an experience and one I shall not forget. I discovered that experience is often what you get after you need it. Complacency and a 'Drop Dead Smile' almost did me in. By the way, the density altitude for that takeoff was 11,500 ft. Looking back at our weight that day, with limited power available, it was sheer madness.

Thinking back to my old mentor's warning of what he called an Aspen Appreciation Event, I remembered his words, "If you are foolish enough to encounter one of your own doing and survive, you will understand my meaning."

My old friend and mentor is no longer with us, but I got it if he is still hovering about it. Thank you, sir! I now completely understand your meaning.

Chapter Sixteen
"DOUBLE TROUBLE"

You've Got to be Kidding!

Traveling the world to exotic locations and enjoying corporate aviation has been a gratifying career. The benefits of a liberal expense account while enjoying an excellent salary were, in a word, outstanding.

As mentioned in Chapter Ten, I was fortunate to become the newest member of what eventually became a multinational company with 12 pilots and three large corporate jet aircraft. I was soon introduced to frequent international flying. Three Hawker and Challenger aircraft were eventually replaced with three Gulfstream aircraft: two G650s, a G450, and a Global Express. Unpredictable and surprising are just two terms that describe many of the 'pop-up' flights and the company's CEO. The only passengers on these trips were often his wife and young son.

One such occasion, I received a call one afternoon to deadhead in a Challenger (No passengers) to Phoenix, where the CEO and his family were staying. They had been flown to Phoenix three days prior and were expected to remain for at least a week. The aircraft was flown back to its home base, and we await the call to return. So, it was a bit of a surprise to get the call to return to Phoenix so soon. Aircraft catering was not requested as standard, which seemed rather odd. It was always asked when the family flew. Fearful it had been overlooked, I was told no catering would be put on board. We were instructed to call upon our mid-afternoon arrival, Phoenix time. The hotel's name, telephone number, and suite were also provided.

As instructed, a call was made announcing our arrival in Phoenix. The CEO answered the call.

"We have arrived at Phoenix's Sky Harbor airport," I said.

"Why are you at Phoenix?"

"We were told you requested a pick-up from Phoenix, as that is where you had arrived three days ago."

"Dammit, I told them that I was much closer to Tucson. Fly to Tucson and call me when you arrive there."

"Rent a car and drive to Harrah's resort in Maricopa. You have my suite number. Come up when you get here." Click!

The call ended with that. Not quite an hour later, another call announced our arrival in Tucson.

It turned out that Harrah's was only about 40 miles or so from Phoenix but almost twice that from Tucson. This was another 'snafu' I was not about to mention to an already seemingly confused and upset CEO. When asked, "What the hell took you so long?" I lied, saying the rental car company was at fault.

Thinking he and his family would return to company headquarters in the Midwest, I was told we were to fly to Aspen, Colorado, instead, with only his young son's new dog. It seems the dog was driving him crazy, and he just wanted to get rid of it.

Yelling for his son to bring us the dog, I was surprised to see it was the size of a small pony—a Great Dane that dwarfed his nine-year-old son. The family was staying; only the dog was leaving.

"Carlos (the houseboy of their Aspen estate) will meet the aircraft in Aspen," he said.

A few hours later, arriving in Aspen, CO., the door was opened. Carlos stood at the base of the aircraft steps with a parrot on his right shoulder. The only thing missing was a hook for his right hand. At this point, not much surprised me. Nonchalantly, I said, "Hi Carlos, here's the dog. What's with the 'Polly' on your shoulder?"

In Spanish-accented English, he replied: "Misses boss lady wan jue to take heem to Key West. Jue weel be met by sumone. Bird ees sik from Alli tude." (The bird had never adjusted to living at an altitude of eight thousand feet and was constantly angry and biting everyone and everything.)

After temporarily securing the dog to the handrail of the aircraft steps, Carlos came aboard and secured the parrot to an armrest of the VIP seat in the cabin. While doing this, and having never been on this aircraft before, he noticed the seats were not made of leather but of a soft material he wasn't familiar with. Asking what it was, I replied, "Mohair."

With a strange look, he said, "Eet mus hab many Moe's for all dees seets."

It had to be one of the funniest lines I have ever heard.

The parrot squawked throughout the flight to the Keys. It pooped all over the costly mohair seat, creating quite a mess for the cabin cleaners when we finally arrived home the next day, having overnighted in Key West.

The company chairman was the founder, and his brother was the vice chairman. They had never flown together on the same aircraft, as each enjoyed his separate jet aircraft. There were always three jet aircraft in the fleet: one for the chairman, one for the vice chairman, and the other for company executives on company business. They were liberally used, often flying just the family members or empty on errands for them, keeping us pretty busy.

Another example I remember flying was a 'deadhead' flight from Aspen, CO, to Palm Beach, FL, to pick up comic books their son had forgotten when he departed from their ocean-side home to their lovely home in Aspen.

While jet fuel was much cheaper in those days, it still cost several thousand dollars an hour to fly, making the dog, parrot, and comic books some of the most expensive on the planet. (I guess they didn't sell those particular comics in the mountain resort of Aspen.) All it takes is a little extra cash!

I was a pilot for this company for fifteen years until the founding chairman turned over the reins to his son. Thereupon, he furloughed (fired) four pilots and sold one jet. I was one of the four released. It was explained that the fairest way to do this was to put two of the highest-paid pilots and two of the lowest-paid pilots on permanent leave, explaining it wasn't personal. "It was a business decision."

Years of loyal service to a company I had been with from almost the beginning meant nothing. However, it was fifteen years of great experience and beautiful memories.

Chapter Seventeen
"BERLIN CORRIDORS"

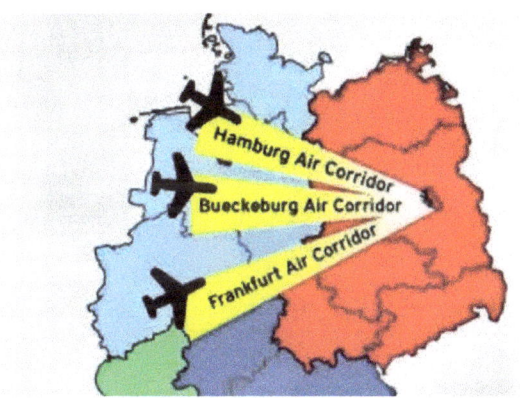

Pushing Through!

World events often move fast, but it is hard to match the famous happenings in recent history. One of the most prominent is the fall of the Berlin Wall in 1989. Built in 1961, the Soviet-led communist bloc had been teetering on the brink of collapse for several years. The demolition of the famous wall helped define a new world order.

Berlin was carved up at the end of the Second World War. The city was subdivided into four quadrants by the British, French, Americans, and, of course, the Soviets, with the Soviets occupying all its eastern part. Each country was responsible for policing its zone or sector of the capital.

In 1948, long before the wall was built, Stalin decided to squeeze the Western Allies where they were most vulnerable.

He cut off all access to West Berlin by road, train, and ship, but not by air. An airborne semi-military operation referred to as

'The Berlin Airlift' took place in response to the Soviets' attempt to starve the city. Dakota aircraft (DC-3s), C-54s (DC-4s), and even two German Junkers Ju-52s were flown, complementing the humanitarian airlift. The resulting routes flown into Berlin later became known as the Berlin Corridors. There were three corridors. In later years, a flight into either of the corridors required flight crews to be fully briefed, certified, and credentialed.

Not long before I was canned from that multinational company, I often found myself in Nice, France, for several weeks on end. The Côte d'Azur served as our European headquarters, from where flights were flown throughout Eastern and Western Europe.

After settling into our hotel after a long flight from New York, I received a call from the CEO. "I need to be in Berlin tomorrow afternoon for a few days. I plan on leaving at 1 p.m."

"We can't," I said.

"Why not?"

"I have not been certified to enter the Berlin Corridors."

"What the hell are you talking about?" he said.

I explained that Berlin lies deep into Soviet territory, over which we must fly. "There are only two places to obtain that certification. Charleston, SC, or Frankfurt, Germany.

I would be happy to catch a flight to Frankfurt or fly our aircraft to Frankfurt and receive the certification briefing from the USAF. I need to know now, as a reservation is required."

"Why didn't you tell me about this sooner?" he said.

Of course, that prompts the question: *'Why didn't he tell me about his plans sooner?'* Employment was essential to me, so I stifled my temptation.

"Get a reservation and get to Frankfurt ASAP. Let me know when it's done." The call ended.

Arriving at Frankfurt Rhein-Main Airport, I caught a cab to the US Air Force base on the opposite side of the field, where I had an appointment with Major Martinez, the Berlin Corridor briefer. The briefing was comprehensive and lasted about two hours. I was given a flight packet containing a briefing pamphlet with hair-raising instructions. It seemed that an interception by a Soviet aircraft was a genuine possibility.

"Not to worry; there hasn't been an interception in a few years. I have flown the corridors several times a month in a military aircraft and have never been intercepted."

He didn't say he had never been intercepted because he was flying a military aircraft.

"Remember to adhere to all instructions strictly. Good luck!"

With that happy admonition and a handshake, I was shown the door. Returning that same evening to Nice, France, I called the CEO. "Got it. When do you wish to leave?"

"Tomorrow at 9 am."

Briefing my F/O that evening, I felt we were ready.

The following morning, a flight plan was filed for Berlin. The Berlin Air Safety Center (BASC) handled flight plans for entry into an air corridor, coordinating with the Berlin Air Route Traffic Control Center (BARTACC).

Berlin Corridors

Three Corridors

"Two Ways in, One way Out."

Speed: "250Kts."

Altitude: "10,000 Ft."

Cleared into the 'Frankfurt Corridor' (the longest) at 10,000 ft, we were instructed to maintain 250 knots strictly. The corridors were twenty miles wide to allow for weather deviation if necessary. The optimum course was to stay in the center. Air traffic control advised us that altitude and airspeed were closely monitored. We were further informed that on this particular day, the Soviets possibly planned flight exercises in the airspace we were to fly through.

Our first entry into one of the corridors, the Soviets picked this day for military exercises. You must be kidding.

"These exercises may or may not take place. If they do, you will be issued an immediate clearance to climb and maintain 13,000. This attitude has been agreed upon and recognized by the Soviets as safe airspace. Monitor this frequency at all times," we were told.

There was so much adrenaline pumping now that if we had lost an engine, we may never have noticed it. Cited below are a few incidents that Major Martinez briefed me on. They took place while we were over Soviet territory and contributed significantly to that adrenaline flush as we entered the corridor.

In 1948, a British Vickers 610 suffered a midair collision in this same airspace as a Soviet pilot performed illegal aerobatics.

In 1952, two MiG aircraft strafed and attacked A Douglas DC-4 (C-54). The DC-4 lost numbers 3 and 4 engines but could land at Berlin's Tempelhof airport. Eighty-nine holes were discovered in the aircraft. There were no fatalities.

In 1966, a Pan American 727 crashed while in Soviet territory. The cause of the crash has never been determined. The black boxes and aircraft control surfaces were never returned by the Soviets, who have consistently denied their involvement in the crash.

There have been several more recent interceptions of commercial aircraft while in the corridors. All were waved off by the Soviet or East German pilots as they saluted after scaring the hell out of unsuspecting crews and passengers.

There were three Berlin airports. Tempelhof, Tegel, and Gatow. Our destination was Tempelhof. (An interesting side note: Tempelhof received its name from the Knights Templar, who occupied this territory in the 13th and 14th centuries.)

While our first foray through this imaginary tunnel proved uneventful, we did pass over several Soviet or East German air

This is a nautical chart of the corridors.

bases. Hind helicopters were stationed on the ramps, and two were seen flying below us. No harassment or military exercises materialized during our transit into or out of Berlin.

Note: the center one is the shortest and is much desired by airlines for fuel efficiency.

The other is an overhead picture of the corridors superimposed on nighttime in East Germany, with an active West Berlin in the circle.

Several additional flights were made to Berlin. They never became routine and were always entered with a heightened focus and all senses on alert.

The Berlin Corridors were decommissioned in 1991, and all three airports they served have also been closed. A new Berlin Airport is located eleven miles southeast of the city center in the Berlin state of Brandenburg. It is named after Willy Brandt, the former mayor of West Berlin and former chancellor of West Germany.

The Berlin Corridors have now been relegated to the archives of history. Memories are constructed of history, and many historical events are memorable. When one is fortunate enough to have been a part of such an unforgettable history, an attachment of humility, pride, and achievement will reside forever in those notable, memorable halls of aviation accomplishments.

Fortunate beyond words, I am a member of a blessed profession.

Chapter Eighteen
"NO CLEAR OPTIONS"

Paris Is Closed!

The advent of spring always signalled a busy flying season for my company. Flights to Europe were flown throughout the year, but increased with the milder seasons.

The Côte d'Azur (The Gold Coast, French Riviera) is a resort area in southern France. From the Italian-French border in the east to Marseilles in the west, it includes the Principality of Monaco with the city of Nice just 9 miles to the west, St Tropez, Cannes, Provence, and several lesser-known towns further west, including Marseilles. It is bordered in the south by the Mediterranean Sea. Nice, and its airport, which serves the eastern portion of the Riviera, also serves as our company's primary destination in France and temporary European headquarters.

It also serves as the 'jumping off' point to other destinations on the continent, with Paris, the 'City of Lights,' often being one of them.

Anyone who has travelled to France, and Paris in particular, may testify to the often-unannounced labor strikes or work stoppages that can and do cripple commerce. Be it trash collectors or construction laborers, but air traffic control professionals?

Our accommodations while in Nice were at the 'Hotel Palais de la Mediterranee,' located along the Promenade des Anglais—English Walkway—facing the beach and the Mediterranean Sea. A beautiful setting. The hotel has since been remodelled and refurbished and is now a Hyatt property. (The Promenade gained notoriety in 2016 when a truck was deliberately driven at revellers celebrating Bastille Day on the Promenade. Eighty-six were killed, and 405 were wounded.) Enjoying a room service breakfast the following morning of our arrival, I received a call from the company CEO. "How soon can we leave for Paris?"

"Give me two hours. Is that soon enough?" I replied.

Snickering, he said, "I knew I could count on you."

All preparations had been completed after a 'rash' of phone calls. The Challenger 601 aircraft was freshly fueled and catered, a flight plan was filed, and all pre-flight checks were completed in record time.

We were soon airborne and on our way to Paris.

As we approached Paris airspace, we were advised to contact 'Paris Control' on their discrete frequency.

"Good afternoon, Paris, Challenger 62MS checking in at Fl 350." (Thirty-five thousand feet.)

"Bonjour, 62MS. Turn right!"

It was an odd and unclear clearance, to be sure. My right seater asked, "What did he say?"

"It sounded like he said turn right," I said.

"And do what?" he asked.

"Ask him," I replied.

"Center, N62MS, Say Again?"

"N62MS, Turn Right or left. Paris is closed."

"And do what? Go where?" we asked.

At this point, another voice came over the frequency, confirming that Paris control was now closed. "We are on strike," said the new voice. "Be advised, all radar control is now unavailable in Paris airspace. Proceed at your own risk. You may descend to a VFR (Visual Flight Rules) altitude and continue or divert to airspace outside Paris Control. Please get in touch with your last air traffic control frequency." (Paraphrasing.)

The exclamation, 'WTF,' doesn't justify our confusion. Checking the onboard computers, we could ascertain that our flight position was less than 80 NM from the French city of Poitiers, just outside Paris' control airspace.

Taking a heading in that direction, we immediately contacted our previous air traffic controller. He instantly cleared us to descend and revised our flight plan for Poitiers with a new heading to fly. Apologizing, he said he had not been informed of the Paris airspace closure as it happened after he initially handed us off to the Paris frequency. Nice that they talk to each other!

Having been to Paris on many previous occasions, I had often witnessed the propensity of the French to call an almost instantaneous strike or work stoppage to demonstrate perceived grievances in many fields of endeavour, regardless of the consequences. I had, however, never in my wildest imaginings considered air traffic controllers calling for an immediate strike or walking out. As we later learned, some supervisors had immediately manned radar scopes unfamiliar to many in management, as they had little current experience working those vacated positions. These marginally qualified supervisors commenced diverting as many flights as possible away from Paris to mitigate the potentially tragic outcome of the strike, ergo, our diversion. As it turned out, the walkout lasted less than two hours. However, commercial air traffic was affected almost all over Europe, including departures from the US, which took several days to return to normal.

A limo was ordered for my passengers, and they were driven to Paris. Poitiers is approximately 215 miles from Paris, or close to a 3.5-hour drive. This occurred in the mid to late 1980s. I have not heard of it ever happening since then.

However, one of my best friends, a captain with USAir who frequently travelled to Paris, mentioned that work slowdowns were often called, causing many delays and holding off aircraft approaching Paris. Ah, the French!

Several other aircraft diverted to Poitiers, and hotel accommodations were suddenly at a premium. We eventually found rooms at a small hotel in the town center square. While checking in, the lady at the front desk noticed that I had a button missing from my shirt. It seemed the wind had blown my tie over my shoulder and revealed this to her. This is significant because a knock on my door came 15 minutes after arriving at my room. It was the same lady. I had just taken my shirt off and placed it on the bed. Pushing past me, muttering something in French, she grabbed my shirt, indicated it was missing a button, and disappeared. Ten minutes later came another knock on my door. She stood with a lovely smile, pointing proudly to the new button she had sewn on my shirt. It was a wonderful and pleasant surprise and gesture. Up until then, I hadn't been too enamoured with the French.

I base that on the often-rude reception from many Parisians. Of course, that also brings to mind many New York City dwellers.

To our delight, the 'Tour de France' was bicycling through the city that afternoon. It was an expected and pleasant event, to be sure.

As a history buff, I was also aware of the Battle of Poitiers that had taken place three miles east and five miles south of the city in the year 1356. This was called 'The Hundred Years War.' There is a 900-year-old cathedral in the town center where the French knights and soldiers prayed before the battle with the English, who defeated the French King Jean II. I was in heaven, surrounded by so much history.

Chapter Nineteen
"TURNING POINT"

What Do You Suppose Happened?

After almost fifteen years with my previous employer, I needed a job. Hired by a Chicago-based financial company, I was told the primary reason for my hiring was my Aspen, CO, flight experience. It was also the location of the Snowmass Land Company, owned by the same Chicago company, as well as the location of one of the CEO's homes.

The board chairman soon decided that my family and I should live in or near Aspen, where he spent much of his time. The company had three bases of operations: Aspen, CO; Chicago, IL; and Van Nuys, CA. The CEO enjoyed a beautiful mountaintop home high up on Snowmass Mountain.

Basing an aircraft in Aspen would require a crew presence. I had to move. Ah, shucks! It was scarcely a hardship.

As mentioned in a preceding chapter, Aspen, CO, lies just under 8,000 ft above sea level. Nestled on the beautiful Roaring Fork Valley floor, gorgeous mountain vistas in all quadrants continually leave one breathless: Red Mountain to the north, Smuggler Mountain to the east, and Aspen Mountain to the south. Other mountains around Aspen are Snowmass, Aspen Highlands, and Buttermilk. The city lies at the base of Aspen Mountain, which is commonly referred to as AJAX.

Aspen Airport's elevation is 7815 ft. The views from any aircraft window are spectacular while descending to the valley floor airport. Jaw-dropping vistas abound as Mother Nature presents her mountains with a kaleidoscope of breathtaking colors during autumn. Glistening snow-covered peaks reflect against an azure sky as formidable slopes beckon ski enthusiasts worldwide during winter. I made my home 'down valley' at Glenwood Springs for nearly ten years.

Any pilot who has flown into Aspen will tell you that it is always challenging, exciting, and, at times, stressful. Several surrounding mountains rise above the airport by six thousand feet in some quadrants, necessitating very high landing minimums during questionable weather events. Visibility on approach to Rwy 15 isn't the only consideration.

Tailwinds on approach above 10 knots should dictate a missed approach or, in some aircraft, a somewhat dicey circling approach to Rwy 33. Rwy 15 is the landing runway, while Rwy 33 is used semi-exclusively for takeoffs. Unfortunately, several aircraft accidents have involved corporate aircraft attempting to land with reduced visibility or experiencing excessive tailwinds.

On February 13, 1991, I was piloting a Learjet 35 from Chicago to Aspen, CO, with our CEO as my passenger. Regardless of the weather conditions, he would continually badger the pilots to violate landing minima and 'get him in.'

Two different views of runway 15. An approach to Aspen in a light snow shower

Weather conditions for our arrival that day were reported as intermittent snow showers, variable low ceilings, and mild winds from the south. Descending from altitude, we were cleared from over Red Table VOR for a visual approach to Rwy 15. Aspen airport was in sight. Suddenly, a very black column of smoke arose near the airport. An immediate clearance was issued to proceed directly to Rifle, CO, as Aspen airport was now closed.

Monitoring tower and approach control frequencies, it was disclosed that a Learjet 35 had just crashed. (The FAA later determined the cause to be the crew's failure to maintain airspeed and control of the aircraft, as well as an unstabilized landing approach after a missed approach due to losing sight of the runway at a low altitude because of a sudden snow shower.)

Advising the CEO we're diverting to Rifle, he came forward and sat on the potty seat behind the co-pilot. Indicating the smoke, I told him the reason for the change. "A Learjet had just crashed near the airport."

"What do you suppose happened?" he asked.

Turning toward him, I said, "Probably some idiot in the back was pushing them to get in."

Slinking to the back of the aircraft, not another word passed between us. Since then, several more accidents have occurred while landing on the approach to Aspen. Two of the more serious ones are recounted below.

The Gulfstream III ricocheted off of the Bluffs, rolling up onto Runway 15

On March 29, 2001, a Gulfstream III crashed on approach to Rwy 15. It was determined that the flight crew's operation of the aircraft below minimum descent altitude without visual reference to the runway was the leading cause of the accident. Eighteen Fatalities.

On January 5, 2014, a Bombardier Challenger crashed upon landing, experiencing a post-impact fire that fatally injured one and seriously injured two others. It was determined that a previous landing attempt had been aborted because of a very high 33-knot tailwind and low visibility. The second attempt in basically the same weather conditions proved fatal. Low-level wind shear had been reported with a gain of airspeed of approximately 20 knots. The tailwind at the time of the crash was reported to be at a steady 33 knots.

Before

After

Oh, I failed to mention that upon landing at Rifle after the Learjet accident at Aspen in 1991, the CEO, having had time to reflect on the crash, said, "Don't ever let me push you guys to get in anymore."

He never did!

Chapter Twenty
"R.V.S.M."

*Reduced Vertical Separation Minimum
Challenge of the Moment!*

The flight department of my new company consisted of two Learjets and an Astra jet, pictured above. One Learjet was based at Chicago's Pal-Waukee Airport, the Astra jet was based in Aspen, and the other was at Van Nuys Airport in Southern California.

The roster included six pilots—two in California, three in Chicago, and one in Colorado, me. It seemed like a problematic arrangement, but it worked just fine. Trips were scheduled in advance, and aircraft and crew were positioned ahead of time as needed. Most trips were domestic, with a few European trips, as the company also had offices in London, UK. Those trips were flown in the Astra jet. On one occasion, however, a 'pop-up trip' to London found the Astra jet unavailable. It was on a 'Road Show' with company executives visiting several cities, while only one of the two Lear jets was available as one was in maintenance.

This was during the years the Concord SST flew the Atlantic. The plan was for the CEO to be flown to JFK on the Learjet. Approaching JFK, a call will be made to British Airways ground control operations to announce our ETA. Parking instructions would then provide a gate number adjacent to the Concord. BA personnel would meet the Learjet, escorting our passengers directly onto the Concord. (A one-way ticket on the Concord to London at the time was about $10K. This helps explain the exceptional service.)

The Learjet would then depart for London carrying the CEO's luggage. The Concord would arrive in London in hours, and the Learjet would arrive the next day. The company owned a fully furnished Condo in London with well-stocked closets. The luggage aboard the Learjet wouldn't be needed until the conclusion of the CEO's business. The aircraft would then be at his disposal to enjoy traveling to various cities and countries in and around Europe for an extended vacation.

The only Learjet available for this trip was the West Coast-based Lear. It was almost due for a serious engine inspection, and the hours flown on this trip would put it right up against its engine inspection due time on its return to the States. RVSM had recently been implemented over the North Atlantic, requiring crew and aircraft to be certified to fly between 29,000 and 41,000 ft in Atlantic airspace. Two of the company aircraft had been RVSM certified. The Learjet we were to fly was not. I saw no problem; Learjets are comfortable flying at FL410 (41,000 ft). This Learjet, however, as it turned out, was not.

Our flight route was from Aspen, CO, to JFK. The flight plan called for stops at Gander, Newfoundland; Shannon, Ireland; and finally, London. The flight was routine to Gander. Attempting to reach FL410 presented a problem. Outside air temperatures at altitude were average at ISA during the first legs of the trip. (ISA is the 'International Standard Atmosphere,' measured at a lapse rate of -2 degrees C per 1,000 ft of altitude. From a baseline temperature of 15 degrees C at sea level) All Learjets loved operating at FL 410, as a rule. This one did not, as it consistently struggled to reach that altitude.

Refueled, we departed Gander and were given clearance to climb to FL410. Initially, the climb was typical, but as we progressed over the water, the outside air temperatures at altitude increased unusually. The increasing temperature considerably reduced our climb rate as the air thinned. This was becoming a serious problem. Barely passing through FL390 (39,000'), the aircraft had slowed from an initial climb Mach number of about .70 Mach and was now at .64 Mach and slowing. A wing stall could occur if the Learjet slowed much more, which would be 'game over.' Coaxing the aircraft, we finally reached FL410, but the outside air temperature was now ISA+12. It was very warm indeed, and we were barely flying at .62 Mach with an unacceptable angle of attack. (Nose high attitude)

The AOA (Angle of Attack) indicator was approaching the danger limit of an impending stall. The right engine, I felt, was the problem, as it was not producing rated power. I tried turning off the right bleed air, which fed air into the cabin for pressurization to help increase thrust, but to no avail. We could not maintain FL410, so we asked Oceanic Control for a lower altitude.

They asked: "Are you RVSM Certified?"

"YES," we lied.

"Standby," they responded.

As the aircraft slowed below .6 Mach, Oceanic responded, "Learjet 35SE, descend and maintain FL290." (29,000')

Dropping the nose slightly, the aircraft fell to 29,000'. We had burned so much fuel in our aborted climb to FL410 that there would be no way we would make it to Shannon, Ireland. We had a tailwind of 60 knots and were hundreds of miles into the Atlantic. A return to Gander was out of the question. Could we make Reykjavik, Iceland? Yes, just barely. Clearance was received, and we turned left and went directly to Reykjavik.

Reykjavik radar identified us at 200 miles and cleared us to descend to FL200. We reported our deficient fuel state and declined the clearance. The weather was good, thank God, as it often wasn't. At about 75 miles, we had the island in sight and began a prolonged descent. A visual approach to an uneventful landing was greeted with sighs of relief. Taxiing in, the fuel gauges read 300 pounds in each wing. (44 gallons.) Less than 100 gallons of fuel were left on board, and who knows if those gauges were accurate in this old aircraft? When hearing of this episode, the Van Nuys crew expressed surprise that we made it, mentioning that the fuel gauges had been extremely inaccurate on the low-end readings. They claimed the gauges had been squawked and would be replaced at the next inspection. It would have been nice to have been verbally advised of this. However, no squawk was found in the logs for either the right engine's low power output or the fuel gauge anomaly. The pilot in charge responded: "Oh, I could have sworn I wrote them up. Guess I didn't."

Chapter Twenty-One
"THE CITY OF TROYES"

The Medieval 16th Century Town of Troyes, Champagne

Unbelievable Kindness!

Trips to Europe were always fun. They required a lot of work and planning, but once there, they were entertaining.

Your private jet was a practical way of visiting several countries, many on the same day, conducting company business. Acquiring the overflight and landing permits required a Herculean effort, making trip planning tedious and fatiguing. Greeted with exhaustion at day's end, a well-deserved meal and a soft bed were always well received.

On one such trip to France's northcentral Champagne region, we visited the ancient city of Troyes (Pronounced: Twah). We expected to remain on the ground for only 4 to 5 hours and then fly to the Côte d'Azur (The French Riviera), landing at Nice.

Before departing Le Bourget, NOTAMs (Notices to Airmen) were checked for the city of Troyes for any remarks of interest. Nothing of consequence was noted. Arriving at Troyes, we ordered fuel and catering for the later flight. All went well until I attempted to pay for the fuel and services with an international Shell Carnet card.

"I'm sorry, Captain; we do not accept credit cards."

"Well, that's no problem, as I have USD in cash."

"I am again sorry, Captain, but we only accept French Francs." (This was before the Euro was introduced as the coin of the realm.)

"I am afraid I have no French Francs, Monsieur."

"Aucun probleme. Un moment." (No problem, one moment) He turned, reached into the cash drawer, and, while handing me 300 francs (about $50), summoned a taxi.

He explained that the money was to pay for the taxi ride into the city, where we would find a bank to convert our USD to francs, with enough left for lunch while in the city. (This was one of the most generous gestures I had ever experienced. Unexpectedly, it took place in France.)

Everyone we encountered on this stop proved courteous and friendly and seemed genuinely happy we were there. None more so than an older couple sitting across the dining room from us at a delightful bistro, where we enjoyed a great lunch in the city center. The old gentleman kept staring at us and smiling. Once catching my eye, he began gesturing and waving his arms as a child might imitate an airplane. We wore our wings and epaulets, so I assumed he acknowledged we were pilots.

Nodding in the affirmative and smiling back at him, he began pointing to himself as if to say, "So am I!"

He spoke no English, but his wife spoke a little, explaining that during WWII, he was also a fighter pilot and that he had shot down three 'Boche' as he called the Germans.

(Boche is an abbreviation of caboche, or bochon, an acronym of cabochon, and is a recognized French word used familiarly for 'head,' especially a big, thick head, {'slow-pate'}.) He then began a 'dogfight' with his hands to explain, in fighter speak, just how he did it. What great fun to see how excited he was to relive that experience. As we paid the check and rose to leave, he crossed the room, hugging us in a beautiful gesture of friendship and camaraderie. I still remember his face. I noticed his eyes were getting misty as he remembered so long ago as we bid them.

"Adieu."

Returning to the airport, I attempted to repay the francs given to us earlier. It was refused with a smile and a "Welcome to

Troyes."

In all my years of experience, I had never been greeted with such respect and warmth as we were that day. The experience we often encountered in Paris was just the opposite.

Chapter Twenty~Two
"CHOOSING SIDES"

The Luck of the Draw!

T he chairman, whom I flew almost exclusively, gradually grew more irascible as the years passed. Several divorces contributed to his ever-increasing foul moods. A series of subsequent girlfriends did little to mitigate his irascibility. Soon, after several years, his abusive behavior toward me and all flight department personnel reached a point where my blood pressure was becoming a significant problem, making it more challenging to acquire the necessary medical certificate to continue to fly. After deliberating with my wife, I decided I should seek employment elsewhere. The impetus that propelled my decision took place one day, as more verbal abuse confirmed my decision.

In 1998, my wife and I left our home in Colorado after several years. Immediately after networking among my peers, I was advised of two exciting opportunities as a corporate aircraft captain: one in Denver, CO, where I would captain a 601 Canadair Challenger, and the other in Hilton Head Island, SC, where I would captain an older British Hawker 700. The Challenger was an obvious better choice for several reasons.

Having experience in both types, we were off to Denver for an interview. The owner of the Challenger was also the company chairman. When scheduling an interview appointment, I was informed that the chairman would be conducting the interview personally. My wife accompanied me to the prospective interview, as we had tickets from Denver for a flight to Savannah, GA, later that day. Another interview had been scheduled with the prospective employer the following day. Savannah, GA, was the closest airport to Hilton Head, SC. Anxious for early employment, I felt that every opportunity should be pursued.

The Denver interview was to take place on the top floor of the tallest building in the city. Arriving at the scheduled time, we were shown into an anti-room and left alone for almost an hour. No amenities were offered, and no soul checked on us during that time. An update would have been nice.

Finally, a man introduced himself as the board's chairman. Ignoring my outstretched hand, he said, "Follow me."

Attempting to introduce my wife, he ignored that overture, turned his back, and walked back through the open door.

This was beginning to feel like a huge mistake.

Once in his office, I was directed to a seat in front of his oversized desk. No small talk, no niceties regarding our trip to Denver, nothing. Instead, he immediately began questioning me on the systems and operation of the Challenger. Scenarios such as: "You are over the Atlantic Ocean when the number two engine fails. What are you going to do?" And: "The aircraft just suffered a major hydraulic failure; what actions would you take?" Electrical failures, control problems, and landing gear issues came at me rapidly.

Finally, when satisfied, he called the hangar at Centennial Airport where the aircraft was hangered and advised that I should be shown the aircraft. Our contact in the field was his long-time flight attendant. Introductions were made on our arrival. Shown onto the Challenger, which was quite a beautiful aircraft, our guide whispered that I should not mention that I was a prospective pilot for the plane. Asking why, she said: "Do you see that man over there by the aircraft Tug? He is the current captain that you will be replacing. He is not aware he is to be replaced very soon."

I asked why and also how long he had been with the company.

She wouldn't say exactly, adding that he had been the captain of the Challenger for more than five years, but she would rather not expound on any reasons the chairman had for replacing him. I felt she knew but wasn't saying. With that bit of info, I took my wife's hand and bid her goodbye.

I wanted nothing more to do with this fellow. This confirmed the bad vibes I had already experienced during our initial meeting.

Arriving at the Hilton Head Island/Savannah airport later that evening, we met my co-pilot of the Hawker that I was being interviewed to fly. Accommodation was made at The Hyatt Resort on the Island, and a luncheon was scheduled for the next day on the pool deck overlooking the ocean. The owner and his wife were delightful and gracious. I did find it a bit strange as the owner had on a straw Panama hat the whole time we were together. As we talked about the opportunity he was offering, he noticed at some point that I was curious about his hat, occasionally glancing at it. He explained that I did not wish to see what he had underneath it, explaining further that he was suffering from a brain tumor and that he had recent brain surgery to remove it, and the chances of his survival beyond two years would be a miracle. He wanted to provide his family with a highly experienced and safe pilot, mainly after he was gone. This news saddened me greatly as I had greatly liked him during that short time.

He was of Indian extraction and was, in fact, from India. He also co-founded a Dallas, TX, company called 'i2Technology.' The aircraft was a very old Hawker model 700, which had until recently been flown by an employee of his company with a commercial license. The owner sent him to flight safety for his commercial-type rating in the Hawker. He had zero jet experience up until that time.

The owner told me he had been frightened a time or two by a few 'hairy landings' as he expressed them to me. Speaking later with the pilot I was to replace, he said that this aircraft was way beyond his experience level and had asked to be relieved of his position. The owner readily and happily agreed.

Very generous remuneration and all moving expenses from Colorado to Hilton Head Island were offered, as well as assistance in buying a home on the island. Was I dreaming? Because of his illness, he insisted that a three-year contract be drawn up, guaranteeing me employment with generous (his words) yearly salary increases, renewable automatically at the end of that period, should he survive that long. If not, his wife could renew it as she wished. Three years of guaranteed employment with generous yearly salary increases sounded good to both of us. (A week later, the Challenger owner called me from Denver, CO, to tell me I had the job. I'm so sorry!)

His Indian name was 'Kana.' All knew him as Ken. He was a wonderful man who lasted almost exactly two years. During that time, I grew to love and respect him enormously. Knowing his time was growing short, he asked me to supply him with options for a newer aircraft for his family. He wanted speed and comfort. The Cessna Citation 10, a jet aircraft type that had only recently been introduced, intrigued him. He ordered one. However, just before the delivery of the aircraft, he took a turn for the worse.

His financial adviser refused to accept the plane based on Ken's orders. Cessna returned all the monies paid to date, withholding 150K as a cancellation fee. Ken was good with that. He wanted that speedy aircraft for himself, not primarily for his family, and he explained that he wanted a jet aircraft with larger cabin space for his wife and two children. The speed he felt was less essential for them, too. He asked me to order them a brand-new Hawker jet, which I immediately ordered. Unfortunately, he never lived to see it.

During our time together, he gave me a BMW M3 automobile as a gift, among many other things. I wasn't his employee; I was, as he often said, one of his family members. He meant it and proved it every day. (A term I had frequently heard from previous employers, which always turned out to be anything but!) The man was generous to a fault! A sweet soul! Two days before he passed, he asked to see me. Arriving at his sickbed, he reached for my hand and said, "Eddie, I love you. Thank you!"

Not long after, Kana closed his eyes forever. So sad!

(Much of my adventures with Ken can be found in my book, "Flying Vagabond," which is available on Amazon.)

"Not to worry, said Kana's wife, "I only intend to fly the new jet domestically."

The Hawker was delivered as promised, on time, and was beautiful. I had designed a unique paint design for the exterior, and the family loved it. I was told the aircraft would be flown primarily on domestic trips. Not!

After flying the new Hawker aircraft for about 50 hours, I was informed that a trip to Italy was planned. "Could we do that?"

Soon, several trips to Italy and other destinations in Europe were flown in our new Hawker 800XP. It is a great aircraft, to be sure, but not quite the aircraft needed for these ocean-hopping flights. Headwinds on the return to the US often presented us with minimum fuel on arrival in Gander, Newfoundland, where another technical stop would be necessary. I explained we were flying the wrong aircraft for these trips, as frequent headwinds returning from Europe had often proved problematic.

Money not being a problem, she said, "Well, find me something else."

We needed a different aircraft to continue these types of trips. I agreed to arrange a Gulfstream V aircraft demo trip to Milan, Italy, from Hilton Head Island with 14 passengers and baggage for our next trip to Italy. The aircraft was most impressive and used only twenty-five hundred feet of the four-thousand-foot-long runway for take-off. Confident that this aircraft would solve our international flying difficulties, I asked the boss lady on landing in Milan how she liked it.

"I hated it."

I was incredulous! "What didn't you like about it?" I asked as we sat in the rear of the aircraft after landing.

"Look," she said, pointing toward the front of the cabin.

"Look at what? I asked.

"It's just a round tube," she said.

"Huh? They are all round tubes. There are no square aircraft," I said.

"Find me something else."

"Yes, ma'am!"

One day, on a later trip in the Hawker, we made a technical stop in Shannon, Ireland. We parked next to a Falcon 900.

"What's that?" she asked.

"A Falcon jet," I replied.

"Do you suppose I could see it?"

"Let me check."

The pilot, it turned out, was an old friend and former crewmate from years past.

"Hello, Eddie," he said.

"You know each other?" she asked.

Surprised, I said: "Sure do."

She asked if she could have a look, and she was taken with it immediately. Turning toward me, she said: "Could you get me a ride in one?"

"As soon as we return, I will request a Falcon demo flight for our next trip."

Excusing myself, I left her on the ramp to speak with the Falcon captain. I was requested to get the passengers' passports stamped.

It wasn't a requirement but just something for 'bragging rights.'

Entering the FBO/Handlers building to inquire about getting

the requested stamp, I explained that I knew it wasn't a requirement as we were passing through, but the passengers would love to be able to prove they had been to Ireland. Greeted with a broad smile, as I am sure it wasn't the first time he had heard that request, one of the fellows behind the counter said: "Yes, Sir Captain. Please follow me. I'm sure Finnegan will be happy to oblige. We will go see Finnegan."

Finnegan's office was located in the main terminal building. It was explained that he was the chief customs officer for the airport. The name on the door read: 'Aidan Finnegan, Chief of Customs.' The office was empty. My guide, swearing softly under his breath, was heard saying, "Finnegan, where the hell are you about to now?

"Come on, I think I know where he might be," he said.

Stepping onto an escalator that traveled up to the next floor, we found ourselves in the main passenger terminal. Looking around, my guide spotted Finnegan sitting at the bar with a half-empty pint of Guinness and an empty shot glass at his elbow. A much older fellow, he had very long, unkempt white hair, a gray, sallow complexion, and deep-set eyes, all of which sunshine was beyond helping. Spying us approaching, a scowl came across his face that would have braced a pit bull to fight.

"Ah, there you are, Finnegan. We have been looking for you. The captain here has a request, "he said.

"Can't ya be leaving a man in peace, O'Reilly? What do you want?" said the old man.

"His passengers have requested an official Irish stamp for their passports. They are just passing through Shannon on a technical stop. Of course, it isn't required, but I told him you would happily oblige."

"Well, that's where you're wrong, Laddie; I won't do it. Now get away and leave me be."

"Finnegan, for the love of the Angels, could you show a bit of Irish hospitality and respect and do the lad a favor?"

"It's not required, and you are interrupting my break time. 'No!' Now go and leave me be."

Finnegan was drunk again!

Turning to me, my guide said, "I am sorry," and we headed toward the escalator again.

He's just a drunken sod whose brother-in-law is in the government and got him his bloody job. He has been a disgrace in it. He spends every free minute at the terminal bar. We aren't all like him. Reporting him does no good at all. I am ashamed and sorry.

"I will have a stamp for your passports back in my office. It won't be official, but it will be something. It will signify our flight operation and say: 'Aviation Services, Shannon Airport, and Shannon, Ireland.' At least it will be something."

I could almost feel his embarrassment as I returned to the aircraft. The passengers, laden with purchases from the duty-free department, returned and were positively giddy when I showed them the stamps on their passports. I explained that while the stamps weren't 'official,' indicating entry to the country, they would prove they had been to Ireland.

I called Falcon Jet Corp. in Teterboro, NJ, and a demo was arranged in a week for an impending trip to California. She loved it. Goodbye, Hawker!

A few months later, I discovered Enron Corp. of California had fallen on hard times and was selling off its aircraft. We made an offer on their Falcon 900EX. SOLD!

Thus began a five-year relationship with that aircraft, the memory of which brings me many smiles. I am afraid the memory of my relationship with Ken's wife does just the opposite. She never reinstated the three-year contract. This young lady was 15 years Ken or Kana's junior and had been his secretary when they met and married. Her father was a retired warrant officer in the Army, and her mother was a German girl her father met while stationed there. Having been raised in a typical middle-income family, the billion-dollar inheritance significantly changed her.

Trips to Eastern and Western Europe became almost routine. Recognizing that so many trips kept me from my wife, she would often ask her to join us on several excursions. All of her expenses were generously paid. One place we frequently visited was Rome, Italy.

One day, when asked if she would like to accompany me on another excursion to Rome, she would say, "Not Rome again."

It seems it all depends on one's perspective.

One particular trip to Europe was quite memorable. Over a few weeks, the itinerary included London, Paris, Naples, and Rome. Our departure date remains embedded in our memory, as it was far from ordinary on several levels. Our usual departure time from Hilton Head was between 4 and 5 am. At the time, the runway at Hilton Head was a mere four thousand feet long. (It has since been extended to five thousand feet.) My principal lady was fond of asking many of her friends on several of these trips. The aircraft accommodated 14 passengers and baggage, frequently challenging our accelerated stop performance.

Once airborne, a mandatory stop was often made at Teterboro, NJ, to upload approximately three thousand dollars' worth of Rudy's Catering, which she loved. Fueling in NJ made the trip to London a pretty easy leg.

On this particular trip, our regular flight attendant had been taken ill. I asked a former crewmate to help locate another one for this trip. After several calls, an airline flight attendant on vacation agreed to the trip. Chicago-based, she arrived the afternoon before the scheduled departure day. Much to my chagrin, I discovered she had never flown on a corporate jet. As she had been recommended by my friend, a corporate pilot himself, I took for granted that she had. Oops!

She had only recently been hired and trained on the Boeing 737 for her airline, which I won't mention here. I did my best to indoctrinate her into the aircraft. Rafts, emergency procedures, safety precautions, and procedures generally require several weeks of training. She seemed much more interested in the aircraft galley. It was too late to replace her. Even if I could, I was committed to my mistake in hiring her.

The trip to NJ was uneventful. Fuel and catering were uploaded, and we were finally on our way. We made 'feet-wet' from Newfoundland when it was requested that a meal service commence. Preliminary snacks and drinks were served, after which a main course was offered.

As the flight progressed, mandatory position reports were made crossing each point in our flight plan. After approaching 30 degrees west longitude, we were about to make our mandatory crossing fix report. HF radio isn't always the most precise or best radio reception, and it took several attempts to make that report. During our several attempts to reach Oceanic Control, I heard my name called from someone in the cabin. Not sure it wasn't my F/O, I turned to see several passengers pointing to the overhead. They were pointing to rather fine vapors of smoke filling the cabin. The position report having just been made, I grabbed my F/O's arm, pointed to the rear cabin, and said, "LOOK!"

He immediately bounded from his seat, pushing past the flight attendant standing at the microwave, and investigated the probable cause.

I asked the F/A, "What are you doing?"

"I am trying to cook this fish," she replied.

"How is that working out for you?" I asked.

"Not very well. The microwave stopped working, but I eventually found 'another switch' for it."

"Another switch?" I asked incredulously.

"Yes, right here."

The 50-amp breaker had popped open. Before our conversation, she had pushed and held it in and was about to try again.

"STOP!" I yelled.

Holy crap! I have discovered the source of the smoke. My F/O, hearing the exchange, immediately checked the area. We were sure she had done some damage to the aircraft, but could not ascertain the extent. It seemed the smoke from her fried brain was also a contributing factor. A few good old Yankee colloquialisms were expressed. The fish remained uncooked, and the hungry passengers, the least of my concerns, remained unfed except for some more snacks. I managed to clear the air in the cabin, and a call via satellite phone was made to Dassault, the aircraft manufacturer.

They advised that we continue to Geneva, Switzerland, as a Falcon Service Center was located there, stating they were too busy to accept us at any service center in France. WTF?

I advised Oceanic that we were reducing speed from .82 Mach to .75 Mach to conserve fuel. (This was a lie.) They weren't entirely happy about this, but they had no choice. We proceeded to London's Stansted Airport as scheduled instead of Geneva, as I wished to get rid of the passengers who all had reserved accommodations.

Approximately 20 minutes or so later, this was heard on HF: "The Concord had just crashed shortly after take-off from Charles de Gaulle airport in Paris, killing all 109 passengers aboard."

The date was Tuesday, July 25, 2000.

That sad event underscored the unawareness of our current predicament loud & clear.

While landing at London's Stansted Airport, much extra time was spent inspecting the aircraft. No apparent damage was noted, and we departed for Geneva, Switzerland. The flight to Geneva was uneventful except for flying at a much slower Mach number in a hoped-for effort to preclude any more surprises.

The aberrant microwave was found to have failed because the 60-cycle inverter cooling fan that provides power to the unit had stopped working. The inverter then became overheated, and the 50-amp circuit breaker that protects the unit popped open, thus shutting it down as a safety measure.

All safeguards at that time were removed once the breaker was held in to operate it. This solitary act could have had catastrophic ramifications, as we discovered in Geneva.

The inverter was located behind the galley. When the galley was removed, the aircraft insulation crumbled to the deck, showing evidence of scorching. The aircraft's outer skin had been overheated, as evidenced by the slightly brown outline of the inverter in the white paint on the outer right side. This had not been noticed in London as it was raining hard then. Had we noticed it, we would not have flown it to Geneva. Some say we should not have flown it regardless after landing in the UK. Perhaps they were correct.

The flight attendant (I use the term loosely) was sent home from Geneva; good riddance. I also had a few choice words with my friend who recommended her. She was beautiful, and he thought I would appreciate that. I didn't understand her stupidity.

Two equally memorable events occurred. One will go down in the annals of aviation history, signaling the death knell for the Concord. The other lives on in memory as the 'Luck of the Draw.'

The author in the left seat in the new Falcon 900EX.

Chapter Twenty~Three
"THE LEARJET SURPRISE"

Fixed base operations or FBOs are aviation service centers at all airports that provide many services, from fueling and refueling all aircraft types to servicing the biffy. Many provide crew rest areas and maintenance, both minor and significant, at airports. Hangar space is also often available, sheltering the aircraft from the weather or during an extended stay. Of course, as you might imagine, these services aren't free and can be expensive depending on the size and type of aircraft or provider.

This brings me to an event at a certain FBO in the Southwest several years ago. After a rather long day of several city visits in the western part of the country, we were happy to reach our last stop before heading home. Directed to parking by a 'Follow Me' vehicle, we deplaned and refueled our Falcon 900EX for our flight back to our home base. My F/O and I decided to watch a movie on the onboard TV as we awaited the return of our pax in about two or three hours. The ramp was very busy and filled with parked aircraft, many of which had their APUs running. (Auxiliary Power Units that provide cooling and electrical power to the aircraft without running the engines.)

A Hawker jet had parked next to us initially, but as he departed, the space was quickly occupied by a Learjet 35, towed into that space by the FBO's ramp people. The Learjet flight crew walked with the aircraft as it was being towed and immediately climbed aboard. As soon as the aircraft came to a stop, it was chalked. Moments later, one of the crew deplaned and commenced what appeared to be a rather hurried aircraft walk-around inspection. Before he completed his inspection, a Limo pulled up, baggage was loaded, and several people boarded the aircraft. Watching this all unfold, we thought it rather unusual; passengers showing up just as the aircraft is towed into position for departure can only mean an ASAP unexpected departure.

Our vantage point allowed us to view Lear's cockpit. As the door was closed, we observed the pilot becoming somewhat animated. Rapid movements of his head, arms, and hands, looking at times out of the windscreen, seemed very unusual. As a former Learjet captain, curiosity got the better of me as I deplaned and stood by my aircraft's nose to observe this strange behavior better. I wasn't disappointed.

Opening the aircraft door, the captain and co-pilot flung themselves off the step. Running to the aircrafts rear, the captain opened the engine cowling of the left engine and staggered backward as though he had been Tasered. Standing there, staring, and cussing a blue streak, he regained his composure, dashing to the other side of the aircraft. Being a 'Nosy Nellie,' I followed at a distance only to hear more cursing and screaming as he opened the cowling. While this was happening, the co-pilot was directed to deplane the passengers. Passing me, some of them were shaking their heads in dismay. The captain, in a huff, was right on their heels.

Here is the rest of the story.

Arriving a week prior, the Learjet was placed in the FBO hangar for safekeeping while the crew flew home to return in a week. This is not particularly unusual, as many corporate aircraft operators prefer to send their crews home on the airlines if an extended stay is planned away from their home base to return later. Round-trip airfare could be much less expensive than paying for an extended crew stay at a high-end resort for a week.

During the Learjet's stay in this particular hangar, two men arrived in what was later described as 'maintenance attire,' claiming to perform maintenance. They had proper identification and were shown in the hangar. With one on each side of the aircraft, they immediately began working on the engines. Being left to their work, they soon departed with a thank you to the FBO desk personnel, taking with them both starter generators, one from each engine. At the time, these generators had a price tag of approximately 35K and could be quickly sold to an unsuspecting operator. The FBO, of course, made good the loss.

I had never heard of such a thing occurring before, and I am not sure it ever had before. Pilots are responsible for their multi-million-dollar aircraft, so this was no doubt a shock to those pilots' systems. Stringent security measures were not employed at this FBO at the time. Since then, many more rigorous security measures have been implemented at many FBOs. Could this happen again? You bet! FBOs and pilots must be constantly on guard against those evil among us!

Chapter Twenty-Four
"A PILOT'S ENIGMA"

U.S. Citizenship
and Immigration
Services

U.S. Customs and
Border Protection

Passports and Visas!

International corporate flying presents many exciting challenges for a pilot. Rules, regulations, the FAA, and EASA (International Aviation Authority) generally depend on the crew's knowledge, training, and compliance. Overflight permits, international flight planning, airspace usage charges, radio frequency usage charges, landing permits, and taxi and takeoff permission slots are just a few of the many stressful challenges.

Passenger cooperation regarding closely choreographed and tightly scheduled departure and arrival times at several European airports presents challenges, like informing a CEO of a multinational company that he or she must arrive at the airport no later than a specific time to avoid severe delays in either takeoff or landing at a destination airport. Often, departure times have approached, but passengers have not. Slot times are forfeited, delays are incurred, and appointments/commitments are missed, resulting in frustration. Generally, these learning events are singular and explicit.

Frequently, being asked to fly Europeans to a different city within their country can lead to severe complications. This is called 'cabotage.' The law prohibits carrying passengers and goods within a country to prevent competition from foreign carriers. Cabotage is illegal and subject to aircraft impounding and severe fines, or worse, levied if discovered.

Having done this a time or two, I had heard that for $4K, you could register a US-registered aircraft in the EU, which would exempt an aircraft and crew from cabotage penalties. I discovered that London, UK, had an aviation office providing this service and all the necessary paperwork. Providing letters to display to the interested parties, should the need arise, was paramount. This need most often occurred in France. A letter written in French was imperative as France was the most restrictive, checking almost all flight passengers arriving from other countries. Many aircraft crews and companies were fined severely when it was discovered that they were violating the rules.

Having all the bases covered for most international contingencies, I relaxed and flew several trips across the pond without incident. I never expected to have a problem entering the United States, however. Let me explain!

Hilton Head Island, South Carolina, my home base airport, once had a relatively short runway of only 4,000 ft. (It has since been extended to 5,000 ft.) Frequent trips to Europe originated from there, generally with 12 to 14 passengers and baggage. This was never a problem for the Falcon Jet 900EX. Departures were planned for and made in the early morning to avoid late temperatures.

On one early morning departure for Paris, a quick stop in New York was planned for the owner's favored aircraft catering. After only a short time airborne, the principal passenger entered the cockpit, requesting that we divert to Dallas Love Field to pick up another passenger. Only five passengers were on board: the woman owner, her two friends, and two sons. Clearance was received, and a left turn was made toward Dallas, TX.

Arriving in Dallas just a few days before, the 15-year-old lad, a friend of her sons, was invited to climb aboard for a return trip to Paris. He was a French citizen who had just arrived in the US aboard American Airlines. He was visiting his parents, who had been living and working in Dallas for quite some time, while he was in school in Paris. The aircraft owner's sons had met him when they attended the same school in Paris the year before. Staying in touch, her sons discovered he was in Dallas and asked us to take him to Paris to escort us around town.

All went well until the return trip from Paris. Stopping to clear customs and refuel the aircraft in Bangor, Maine, things went to hell in a hurry.

A US Customs and Immigration vehicle arrived alongside the aircraft. A customs officer walked up the steps of the aircraft, followed by a rather Portly Lawn Troll of a person whom I suspected escaped from a darkened garden somewhere. He was dressed as an immigration officer. There were no pleasantries exchanged, as both men were all business. In the beleaguered voice of a man who would rather be somewhere else, the Lawn Troll called out: PASSPORTS!

All was in order until the French kid presented his passport. "Your French?" said the Troll.

"Oui," said the lad.

"Where is your visa?" asked the Troll.

"I have no Visa. I do not require one."

"Oh, but you do," said the Troll.

Addressing me, he said, "Captain, you have an undocumented alien on board. You have two options. Take him back to France, or I will issue a violation for 5,000 dollars, which will be paid in thirty days."

I explained that the boy had arrived in Dallas, TX, ten days prior on American Airlines without a visa. He had no problem entering the country then. "Why now?"

He extracted a US Customs handbook from his valise and handed it to me, saying, "You haven't read this. I suggest you do so."

He explained that when a citizen from France or several other friendly countries arrives on our shores as a passenger aboard a US flag carrier, they do not require a visa because of international contractual agreements between the airlines and the State Department. "That agreement does not extend to foreign nationals arriving on corporate aircraft."

Electing to accept the less expensive alternative, he happily started writing the citation. Frowning mightily and unsmiling as I assumed only a troll could manage, he handed me the citation and wished us a nice day as both officers departed.

The boss lady was livid! Addressing me, she angrily said: "Why didn't you know that? I'm not going to pay this fine! You are."

I was entirely surprised by this event. The next day, I found a phone number for the State Department. I made the call, hoping to plead ignorance and offer a heartfelt "MEA CULPA."

After frustrating transfers to several departments, I finally reached the correct individual. Explaining the sad tale for his benefit, he began clattering away on his computer, eventually finding the citation issuance. Accepting and understanding the explanation of my ignorance of this obscure anomalous regulation, an agreement was reached with a promise of a more diligent approach to my responsibilities as an international corporate captain. The fine was waived. However, a warning was issued against further violations; my name and aircraft registration number have been flagged.

After phoning the owner with the good news, she told me I had saved myself 5,000 dollars. "This was your fault. I wasn't about to pay that fine!"

Experience is that marvelous thing that enables one to recognize a mistake when one makes it again. It often seemed that the aircraft owner was the most significant challenge I had during those years. As mentioned earlier, corporate aviation does present some unique challenges at times. Despite them, however, I highly recommend it. After all, seeing the world all expenses paid has a certain appeal.

Chapter Twenty-Five
"CAUGHT IN A JAM"

Ah, the Brits!

It had been a very long day. I started in Paris at 6 am, then went to Naples, Rome, and finally to London's Stansted Airport. On arrival at Stansted, the aircraft was boarded by three British Customs and Immigration agents, dressed in what appeared to be military uniforms. They presented their credentials, which stated who they were and what agency they were with. They were all non-smiling, strictly business individuals.

The aircraft was a Falcon 900EX. It had a spacious front galley with a well-stocked and well-imbibed bar. The taller of the agents, about 6'4", asked: "Captain, why isn't the bar sealed and locked?"

I was unsure what he was asking, so I asked him to explain why that was necessary.

"It is a regulation in the UK that all alcoholic beverages be stowed and sealed upon entering UK airspace for an extended stay."

"Sir, I had been to Gatwick and Heathrow in times past and had not encountered that regulation."

His response: "You were fortunate. No matter, here are the seals. Stow the bottles in a lockable cabinet and place these seal locks on it, or it will all be confiscated."

There was no choice there, as this guy wasn't playing around. In the meantime, my passengers were being slightly harassed by the immigration guy. One of the passengers was an Italian who enjoyed dual citizenship with the UK. Thinking he had a violation that would impound the aircraft for violating the cabotage rules, the immigration guy wasn't having any of it until the passenger called his London office. His vice president, a former British policeman, convinced him of my passengers' 'bona fides.' That seemed to mollify the jerk, and we were finally cleared for our two-day stay in London.

On the day of departure, the flight attendant needed to stock the galley with food for the long return trip to the States. Rather than order it from the airport caterers, she wanted to pick fresh food from Harrods department store, which had a magnificent fresh food gallery for some shopping and, of course, to help her lug it all back to the aircraft. Many hundreds of British pounds later, we loaded the Volvo station wagon with the assistance of our driver and proceeded to the Dorchester Hotel in downtown London, as we had been requested to pick up two of our return passengers' luggage and deliver it to the aircraft. Three crew and baggage, several boxes and bags chock-full of groceries; there was barely room for us as we scrunched into the seats. Our driver said not to worry, as the Volvo had a luggage rack on top of the vehicle where he could secure the additional luggage. The car was undoubtedly overloaded as it seemed to bottom out over a few bumps on our trek to the airport.

Arriving at the airport gate, we were escorted into the main building, where we were scanned for weapons. The driver and Volvo were not checked or even asked to enter the building. That same nonsmiling, 6'4" customs guy was one of the few agents seeing our return. I said, "Hello again!" No response and, of course, no smile. Finally cleared, we exited the building again to be crammed into the Volvo. An airport escort vehicle was waiting beyond the barrier to guide us. That's when I let my mouth overload my ass!

Looking at the flight attendant, I said, smiling, "Did you pack the Uzi?"

Attempting humor as no one had inspected the vehicle, just us. Oh shit! Unbeknownst to me, the big customs guy heard it behind me. The flight attendant turned a shade of gray as my co-pilot pointed over my shoulder.

"That tears it! All of you, back inside. Driver, unload the vehicle for inspection. Captain, come with me."

Entering the building and mentioning to his fellow agents what he had just heard, he turned, escorting me into a small room with a table and chairs. Told to sit, he scolded me, reminding me of some old British movies where the old, seasoned sergeant major chews the hell out of his troops. Attempting to apologize, explaining it was just an unfortunate flippant remark, as the car was never inspected and could be carrying anything. Well, he didn't much appreciate that either. I should have just quit while I was ahead and zipped it.

After several minutes of this and the promise of a visit to "the Old Bailey," the London court, if this were ever to happen again, I was released. While this was happening, reinforcements had been called to tear the Volvo apart while searching for anything suspicious. Of course, they knew they would find nothing, but they were transmitting a message that was received loud and clear: don't mess with these guys!

My crew refused to speak to me for hours afterward, except for necessary communication. The flight attendant was particularly peeved, promising she would never fly with me again. My first officer stayed pissed off at me for days. As we were several hours early for departure, this little 'dust up' caused no departure delays for us. The F/A was a contract gal who soon forgave me and flew several more trips. It's incredible what a few happy hour drinks will do!

Chapter Twenty-Six
"BAYLOR THE SAILOR"

T he Ancient and Secret Society of Quiet Birdmen is an international group of pilots dedicated to the mutual good fellowship of all airmen. The QB governor of our local SC hangar is a fellow named Baylor O'Cain. Baylor has always been a source of amusement. His sense of humor and broad smile were as contagious as his wit and personality. He has often been heard whining about his love life or lack of it, much to the amusement of all within hearing. While lady trouble was a familiar subject among most, Baylor's ventures into that arena deserve a notable mention. Many a skirt had left him in the dirt.

In keeping with that theme, let me introduce you to our governor and his travails. Much of the following is secondhand info at best and a bit of 'Scooby Bloody Do' (as my British friends would say). At worst, I present my gift here to our dear old Baylor.

"Baylor the Sailor"

Baylor wanted to be a sailor, plying the oceans wide, but Baylor had a problem that often made him cry.

You see, he couldn't find a woman, no matter how hard he'd try.

A Navy tradition as sure as the tide, a girl in every port promised a hell of a ride.

A girl in every port, true for so many, could leave poor Baylor sad—not getting any!

So, no Navy for him, his chances too slim, his prospects, once hopeful, now proved dim. He soon took to booze, to assuage his blues, A day late and a dollar short, poor guy just missed his cues.

Melancholy and sad, drinking beer after beer, soon walking a problem, he fell on his ear.

One day, in a stupor, a sudden flash did occur, leaving him gasping: that flash just a blur.

Glancing upwards while shifting his eyes, there, far above him, a trail in the skies,

A fast-moving aircraft marking the blue. "A sign," he said, "Now that I can do!"

No women involved, but how to begin? Where to start, where to check in?

An airport, of course, with lessons to learn. "I know the women will come with the money I earn!"

"Pilots get women, everyone knows; being a sailor now somehow just blows!"

A license to fly, an aircraft to own, a thrill of which he had never known.

All types of women, no need to discern, he hoped, with enough money now to burn.

"All would be well, no longer sad; I will bring them all on, the good and the bad!"

The years passed, leaving Baylor confused. What he hoped would happen had left him abused.

Oh, many women beat a path to his door. He found most to be just a bore. So many women, so many obscure, except for one; he needed a cure!

Crabs, the vernacular, laid him low; his recovery, not fun, was very slow.

A change was needed; of this, he was certain. It was time in his journey to close that damn curtain.

An airport friend, seeing he'd become jaded, suggested a place where jokes were traded.

"We meet once a month at a place called Bella's. All of us, you see, are really good fellas.

All pilots, all with career, some doctors, some lawyers, all men of good cheer."

In time, after voting, he was finally accepted; Baylor, now happy, was quite affected.

His initiation was fun; he was happy, excited. His attitude shifted, his thoughts finally righted.

Initiations are secret stuff not spoken of here,

As the penalty, you see, is rather severe. You must be a member to chew on that bone.

The Ancient and Secret Society of Birdmen is now the place Baylor calls home.

NO MORE WOMEN, NO MORE TO ROAM!

Was the above truth or true fiction?

Only those who know him can make that distinction.

Once, a health issue caused his family some grief.

A lack of oxygen was the belief.

His heart had quit pumping, his family's shoulders

slumping.

Heart rates increased, adrenaline jumping. Chances were slipping, his prospects dim,

When a thumping sound caused the doctor to grin.

Born again and loving each day,

It was then that Baylor learned to pray.

Brain damage was feared, the common consensus, Baylor pulled through with all his senses.

No damage here to this man of hopeful good cheer!

Come on, Baylor, it's time for a beer!

Chapter Twenty-Seven
"DO YOU MISS FLYING NOW THAT YOU'RE RETIRED?"

I miss the days when I had to use superior judgment to avoid using superior skill to save the day! I retired in 2019 after more years than I care to remember. For the last several years of my career, I was employed as a simulator instructor for several models of the Hawker jet. Employed by CAE near Morristown, NJ, in 2008, I was destined to spend the next eleven years 'flying the box.' I have flown many different aircraft types and hold twelve type ratings, of which the Hawker jet is the aircraft I have the most time flying in, thus eventually becoming an FAA-designated check airman in that type.

I was not anxious to experience retirement, but old Father Time brings reality home. Thousands of hours in the air have given way to many more hours of writing, reading, and the tube. There had to be more to retirement than just that. As a member of the Ancient and Secret Order of Quiet Birdmen, I decided to put together a PowerPoint snapshot presentation of my long aviation career. Having written a book called *"Flying Vagabond,"* chronicling many of my often adrenaline-filled adventures, I approached a few QB hangars with an offer to present several of those adventures to their membership.

During the early years of my career, I experienced airline flying, but I was not enamoured of it, so I left it when I discovered corporate flying. Enjoying all-expense-paid trips to exotic locations for fifty-plus years suited me much better. A step up in adventure, if not in remuneration, was much more to my liking.

I was filled with trepidation during my first presentation to a large group of almost exclusively retired airline pilots. A bad case of nerves and a somewhat shaky presentation to an intimidating crowd were rewarded with a grateful and appreciative round of applause.

The presentation has improved and grown over the years, as have those groups I have presented to, including several EAA chapters, The Citadel Cadets in Charleston, SC, the University of South Carolina, several flying clubs, and CAP Wings. I am often asked after a presentation, "Do you miss flying now that you're retired?"

I do, of course. On occasion, I still managed to get into the air with a friend who graciously invited me along on several trips he had flown, which allowed me to fly the aircraft. No longer flying because I have to, but rather because I want to, is gratifying.

That question is asked so often that, during my presentations where many of the attendees are airline pilots, I say that I no longer mention I miss it, especially around my wife. Here is why:

We have a cockpit mock-up in our house. When I tell my wife

I miss flying because I was retired, she puts me in the mock-up around bedtime for 8 hours. She has a chair in a closet, turns on the vacuum cleaner to simulate cockpit air noise, dim night light to simulate cockpit lighting, and serves lukewarm chicken with cold vegetables on a tray. When I get sleepy and attempt to doze off, she knocks twice loudly on the door to simulate the F/As entering the cockpit. Then, after 6 hours, she turns on a floodlight directly in front of me to simulate the sun coming up when approaching 20° West. I then get coffee from the coffee maker left on all night.

Finally, she let me out, and I had to get in the backseat of her car while she ran morning errands to simulate the bus ride to the hotel. When we get home, I tell her I'm ready for bed, but the bedroom door is locked, simulating the hotel rooms not being ready. When I promise to never complain about being retired, I am allowed to enjoy my "layover" and go to bed.

Oh, and one more thing: she talks to her friends loudly outside the bedroom door to simulate the hotel maids chattering away in the hall in their native language. After two hours of sleep, she calls the phone beside the bed from her cell and says, "This is crew scheduling; the airline declared bankruptcy today. Sleep tight, honey!"

This has proven to be a very effective reminder of those many 'in late, out early' trips that ring so true for so many! Now that I am home more, my wife wants more attention. One day, she asked me to take her to a place where they make food right in front of you. I took her to Jersey Mike's. That's how the fight started.

I am at a place where doing errands is starting to count as going out. We ended up going to a marriage counselor who was also a therapist. I didn't think the therapist was supposed to say

"WOW" that many times in our first session, but here we are!

I needed a change. I didn't think I had any physical limitations, so I bought a membership in a local gym one day. I was assigned a personal trainer. It's probably my age that now tricks people into thinking I am an adult. After the first session, I ran to the men's room, where the trainer found me crying.

"What's wrong?" he asked.

"I am not going to let you hurt me like that ever again."

"It was one sit-up. You did one sit-up!" he said.

I canceled my membership, and now I am back writing, reading, and watching the tube. I also still give the occasional presentation. Things are finally back to normal. Retired life suits us both just fine.

Happy wife, happy life!

Chapter Twenty-Eight
"PAINTING WITH SAUCE"

Meatball Melodrama!

Just a few months before my retirement as a designated FAA check airman at CAE (Canadian Aviation and Electronics) in Morristown, NJ, I was on a break from a simulator session. Discovering spaghetti and meatballs were on the lunch menu in the cafeteria (my favorite), I decided to order them and planned on taking them home at the end of the day. I had little time to eat it then.

The young lady who was the server, remembering spaghetti was one of my favorites, was overly generous, doling out an extra-large portion. Instead of the usual three large meatballs, I ended up with six and a hefty helping of pasta. This was placed in a large Styrofoam container. (It was not large enough, as it turned out, as it stressed the sterile foam to the max.) That is where the adventure began.

Rushing upstairs and placing the container on my desk, my haste caused it to open slightly, spilling a good portion onto my newly arrived FAA LOA (Letter of Authority, the Fed's approval of my authority to check and instruct), which had just been placed there by the training manager. Scraping this mess back into the container with my hand, some pasta dropped onto the floor with a couple of meatballs. I did my best to clean it, but it did little good as it still left a mess. I hurried to the men's room to clean up my shirt and trousers, which had also been splashed.

While hurrying to the simulator, I explained to my clients why I looked like Emeril Lagasse had just thrown up on me. During the sim session, one smart-ass said, "You smell good enough to eat." Cute!

At the debrief after the simulator session, I once again attempted to clean the mess at my desk before leaving for my apartment. The meal looked viable, as the container was almost full of spaghetti. The ride home was uneventful. I placed the container securely on the passenger-side floor, taking great care. Arriving at my building, I hurried to my apartment on the second floor of the old firehouse in Basking Ridge, NJ. (Built in 1914) I discovered that painters were busily painting the molding and trim on each side of the stairwell and the hallway leading to my apartment. The landlord had hired painters to spruce up the property that day. There were two of them, a young lady and an older man. They were dressed in white painter's clothes. Sprawled about halfway up (or down) the stairs, slouching, each rested on an elbow as they painted.

Carrying my briefcase in one hand while attempting to balance my dinner in the other delicately, I excused myself, proceeding up the 22 steps. Passing the young lady, the Styrofoam container started to bend under the weight, opening and spilling its contents of pasta and meatballs, accompanied by a delicious sauce, onto the stairwell. Watching in horror, three meatballs, propelled by my attempts to keep from dumping them, bounded merrily toward the unsuspecting duo, picking up speed with each step, bouncing ever higher. One of the meatballs struck the young lady just below her throat area, above her shirt opening, lodging itself nicely in the canyon of her exposed cleavage. Unfortunately, she had, at that precise moment, leaned forward to examine her work.

The two other errant balls careened toward the man, splashing into his paint tray, depositing paint onto him, the step carpeting, and his partner. The other continued its trajectory to the bottom of the staircase, resting on a white drop cloth while pasta sauce splashed on the freshly painted walls above the step molding. I was a big hit with these folks. My leather briefcase, which I had dropped, was stopped from sliding down the steps by my foot to limit the damage of my spaghetti spill.

Apologizing profusely, I sheepishly attempted to gather my dinner with my hands, scraping the residue into the container. Offering to assist in removing the meatball from the young lady's chest cavity was greeted with derision. She was already in the process of a 'deep ball extraction.' They both were shocked and as pissed as I was embarrassed.

Finally, collecting the errant meatballs and scooping as much of the pasta as possible, I grabbed my briefcase and fled up the remaining steps. Reaching my apartment door, I carefully placed the briefcase on the floor. Struggling to extract the key from my thoroughly stained trousers, guess what? That freaking container, now somewhat heavier on one side due to the hurried scraping of pasta, opened and dumped pasta, sauce, and one meatball and, once again, splashed on the freshly painted wall in the hallway. The guy, hearing my cussing, investigated. Arriving on the scene, I had no doubt he was contemplating murder.

Apologizing again, I scrapped and corralled the 'f***ing meatball.'

Now my door open, I hurriedly fetched cleaning supplies and attempted to clean everywhere except the young lady. This just made things worse. The wall needed repainting, which I offered to do but was told to "get out of the 'f***ing' way."

As they were finishing up sometime later, I overheard the guy referring to the 'asshole and his f***ing spaghetti.' Yup, I deserved it. The whole thing made me mortified, embarrassed, humiliated, and incredibly humbled. Looking back, it would have been hilarious if it had happened to someone else.

Hearing a mouthful from the painters later that day, the landlord good-naturedly advised me that I had to pay for their overtime. I suggested I treat him to some spaghetti and meatballs.... You can't make this shit up!

Chapter Twenty~Nine
"LET ME TELL YOU A STORY"

KALITTA AIR

How do you build an airline? With a well-thought-out business plan, hard work, determination, and a never-to-be-forgotten daily prayer to the sky gods.

Remember KIWI AIRLINES based at Chicago Midway airport? They had early moderate success until they didn't. Three former Eastern Airlines pilots put their collective heads together with what appeared to be a sound business plan. The airline failed. The best-laid plans, etc., etc. Stories abound as to why it failed, but the bottom line is that it did.

Everyone knows JetBlue Airlines. They are a remarkable exception to the rule: "How do you make a small fortune in aviation? Start with a large one!" One of the founders instrumental in putting JetBlue on the map recently told his story of the airline's success. It is an entirely different one. They are doing very well. Aviation, in general, is very fickle.

After the 'War To End All Wars' ended in 1918, many visionaries, former wartime pilots, rushed to fill the need for air travel. Barnstormers enthralled crowds with rudimentary aerobatics, taking the bravest onlookers up for a small gratuity while others went into debt founding airlines such as American, TWA, and United. Many of those same barnstormers are credited with successful airline inceptions. However, many failed, leaving many hopeful entrepreneurs broke and disheartened. Airline failures, then and now, beg the question: why bother when looking good on paper is often just that? Fortunately, we have all benefited from those who pressed on against the odds.

In the sixties, I often noticed a young fellow diligently loading automotive cargo into a Cessna 310 aircraft at Detroit's Willow Run Airport. He would then climb aboard and fly the aircraft single-pilot in often seriously degraded weather to various destinations. His Cessna 310 eventually gave way to a Twin Beech 18 aircraft. This young man and his Twin Beech would be seen in Detroit, Cleveland, Kansas City, St Louis, and many other cities where automotive factories, primarily the Big Three, were located. I continually marveled at his determination, single-handedly loading cargo aboard his aircraft and flying it to his destination, where he often singularly unloaded it.

Acting as his own freight forwarder, cargo loader, and pilot, his work ethic, diligence, and focus demonstrated a strong desire to succeed and were unparalleled. He was an expert at driving a forklift, gingerly placing a pallet or two aboard the Beech and often removing them at their destination.

"Who is that guy?" I asked one day.

"Oh, that's Connie Kalitta," I was told. "He's also a Top Fuel

Drag Racer."

In 1967, Connie Kalitta Service and Kalitta Air Services were born. As time has proven, this modest beginning had enormous potential.

One of my earliest memories of Connie was his arrival at Detroit's Willow Run Airport in 1967, flying a brand new Volpar Turbine Powered, Tri-Gear Twin Beech aircraft. He was like a proud father to his newborn. Loading the aircraft cargo himself, he was always anxious to show off his proud acquisitions and much-touted and improved takeoff performance. Electing to use Rwy 36 for takeoff at Willow Run (The less-used runway at the field primarily because of its roughness) also provided the best view to anxious onlookers as it ran parallel to the freight hangars. (Rwy 36 was eventually closed.) What was to follow was unfortunate.

Much anticipated, the high-performance night takeoff commenced. Landing lights illuminated the runway, takeoff power was added, and the aircraft began its takeoff roll. Initially, it bounces slightly upon the rough surface, increasing proportionately to the speed. No doubt, believing the aircraft airborne as it bounded against the undulating surface, the gear was raised prematurely. The heavily loaded aircraft, not quite flying, settled onto the runway, displaying two very bright concentric circles of sparks. Emergency vehicles were dispatched to the scene. Unhurt, Connie was later brought to the freight hangar and given a well-deserved round of applause for surviving the accident and the entertainment value of the much-appreciated high-performance takeoff. The aircraft, soon repaired, became a late-night fixture of one man's determination.

Connie loved speed. As a Top Fuel Dragster racer, he raced from the 1950s through the 1990s, dividing his time between growing his airline and Top Fuel racing. His racing bio reads, "The first driver of a Top Fuel Dragster to hit 200 mph in a National Hot Rod Association-sanctioned event – the 1964 NHRA." He raced as 'The Bounty Hunter.' Teaming up with Shirley (Cha Cha) Muldowney, they ran together as 'The Bounty Hunter and The Bounty Huntress' in a pair of Mustangs under the banner of Kalitta Motorsports. Stepping away temporarily from racing in 1971 to concentrate on his aviation business, he was not one to forsake one passion for the other; he returned to racing in 1977 as Muldowney's crew chief.

"The Bounty Hunter"

1978 saw him step into a Top Fuel dragster, the first Top Fuel racer to hit 290 mph. Connie went on to win ten NHRA national events and was inducted into the Motorsports Hall of Fame in 1992. Connie's son, Scott, was also a Top Fuel and Funny Car (Nitro) dragster. In 2008, tragedy struck. Scott sadly was fatally injured during the final round of qualifying at Old Bridge Township Raceway Park in Elizabeth, NJ. When his engine exploded, his funny car was traveling well over 300 mph.

In 1984, Kalitta Air Services became American International Airways, serving several cities from its hub in Philadelphia, PA. In the 1980s, the Kalitta brand appeared on many of the company's cargo aircraft. AIA declared bankruptcy in 1984 and ceased operations in September of that year. Kalitta, however, continued using the AIA name as Kalitta/American International Airways for cargo-only flights until 1997.

In 1990 and 1991, Kalitta/AIA flew 600 missions in support of Operation Desert Shield and Desert Storm. In August of 1993, Kalitta/AIA suffered its first accident when a Kalitta/American International Airways DC-8 struck level terrain 1,400 ft west of the runway at Guantanamo Bay, Cuba. The accident was attributed to an exhausted crew stalling the aircraft in a highly banked turn to the final approach. All three crew members survived the accident. The aircraft was totaled.

In 1997, AIA merged with Kitty Hawk Airlines. Connie resigned to start Kalitta Aircraft Leasing, which bought, sold, and leased aircraft. In April 2000, Kitty Hawk Airlines ceased operations. Connie decided to rescue it. The resultant new airline, Kalitta Air, was born using the operating certificate and assets of the former airline.

Today, Kalitta Air supports the cargo needs of countries from Europe, the Middle East, the Orient, and beyond. Supporting the needs of the Department of Defense Air Mobility Command and the Department of State, Kalitta Air was employed to evacuate US nationals from Wuhan during the outbreak of the COVID-19 pandemic. The National Museum of American Diplomacy's collection of artifacts includes a commemorative plaque honoring the 'Wuhan Evac Team,' featuring a Kalitta Air aircraft with the four Boeing 747 aircraft registration numbers engraved with the dates 01-27-20 to 02-08-20.

From driving a forklift and loading his aircraft to climbing into the cockpit semi-exhausted and flying the aircraft to its destination, where he would unload it, he was never concerned with what other pilots thought of his singular freight operation; he pressed on, knowing in his heart of hearts that he was a winner, and we all know that they never quit!

As the years progress, the memory of that young man remains burned in my psyche. At age 85, Connie still holds tightly to the reins of his creation.

Remember that vision you had and the goals you set for yourself all those years ago, Connie?

Congratulations, Sir! You made it!

Chapter Thirty
"THE CONCORDE AND PEPSI BLUE"

After nearly 50,000 flights carrying 2.5 million passengers, everyone remembers the supersonic Concorde. It holds a special place in history. In 1996, Pepsi-Cola, Inc. approached the British and French to assist them in a promotional and marketing campaign incorporating a Concorde aircraft painted in the Pepsi-Cola colors.

Pepsi planned to paint a Concorde aircraft in the colors of Pepsi-Cola and their new Pepsi Blue cola and fly the aircraft around Europe and the Middle East, but never to the United States. The British immediately refused, dismissing the idea. On the other hand, the French seemed eager to hear Pepsi's proposal. Negotiations finalized, and aircraft registration F-BTSD was delivered to the paint hangar at Toulouse, France, for her new livery. She would fly as a call sign: 'Sierra Delta.'

The chosen aircraft's first flight was on June 26, 1978, from the same Toulouse factory. It was also the same aircraft that holds the world record for flying worldwide in both directions: westbound in 32 hours 49 minutes and 3 seconds on October 12/13, 1992, and eastbound in 31 hours 27 minutes and 49 seconds on August 15/16, 1995. It was also the only Concord to land in Central America, setting a new time record between Juan Santamaria International Airport and JFK.

The Pepsi Concorde operation was to be undertaken secretly, as Pepsi wanted to keep all the surprises for when it unveiled its new identity. 'Pepsi Blue' Concorde 'Sierra Delta' was thus covered by brown wrapping paper after painting, allowing as few people as possible to become aware of the new paint scheme. The aircraft lent itself well to its new blue and white colors so familiar to Pepsi-Cola lovers. Due to heat build-up at higher speeds, the wings were required to remain white because of the lower heat transference of the lighter color. The aircraft would be restricted from flying at Mach 2.02 for only 20 minutes because of the higher speed of heat build-up; however, it was allowed to be flown at Mach 1.7 without restriction.

It eventually left the hangar on March 31st during the night and was quickly rolled to the runway, where it took off for London's Gatwick Airport (LGW), where Pepsi planned to invite its guests to the special launch event. (This is where I first saw the aircraft.) The new drink, Pepsi Blue, was to be launched at Gatwick Airport, revealing the Concorde brand with the color and logo of the product. The Concorde was immediately towed to the hangar after it arrived at Gatwick and made ready for the show. The show took place on April 02, 1996, with Claudia Schiffer, Andre Agassi, Cindy Crawford, and hundreds of journalists invited by Pepsi for the event.

The branding of the aircraft was estimated to cost USD 20 million. 'Sierra Delta' started a promotional campaign in Europe and the Middle East. There were 16 flights, including ferry flights from Orly Airport. Ten cities were visited. Each flight, except the first and last one, had flown supersonic. The promotional campaign, while expensive, served Pepsi well, as sales of their new Pepsi Blue Cola easily surpassed their expectations. The total cost of the venture, which lasted well over a year, is said to have been approximately USD 500 million. If true, one wonders how much Pepsi Blue would have had to have been sold to break even on the venture.

The Pepsi Blue Concorde, F-BTSD, was retired to the Musée de l'Air at Paris-Le Bourget Airport on June 4, 2003, after flying 12,974 hours. Also at the same museum is aircraft F-WTSS (production designation 001), the first Concorde to fly on March 2, 1969, and retired on October 19, 1973, having made 397 flights covering 812 hours, of which 255 hours were at supersonic speeds.

This same aircraft, Concorde 001, was modified with rooftop portholes and observation equipment for the 1973 solar eclipse mission. Its flight over Africa, lasting 74 minutes, became the longest solar eclipse observation. It remains in its solar eclipse mission livery, complete with portholes.

If you find yourself in Paris, the trip to Le Bourget Airport and the Musée de l'Air is worth visiting these beautiful historical aircraft.

As previously stated, on July 25, 2000, I flew a Falcon 900EX from Hilton Head Island to Paris, France. We had just made a position report passing 30-west longitude in the center of the Atlantic Ocean when a transmission announced the crash of Air France Flight 4590. (At the time, we were also experiencing an onboard event of smoke in the cabin. Fortunately, the cause, while discovered, still filled us with trepidation about possible damage to the aircraft.)

Air France Flight 4590 (registration F-BTSC) crashed, departing Charles de Gaulle in Paris, killing all 109 people aboard and four on the ground. It was the only fatal Concorde accident during its 27-year operational history. In the wake of the disaster, the entire Concorde fleet was grounded. All aircraft soon returned to service on November 7, 2001, following the implementation of various modifications to the airframe, which improved their safety.

The crash was eventually determined to have been caused by FOD (foreign object debris) on the runway. A torn metal strip from a departing aircraft was found on the runway and was believed to have been run over by the Concorde during the takeoff roll, bursting a tire, the debris of which punctured a fuel tank, sparking the fire. (A 30-centimeter, 12-inch, spacer that usually keeps the left main landing gear in alignment had not been replaced after recent maintenance; the Bureau of Enquiry and Analysis for Civil Aviation Safety, BEA, concluded that this did not contribute to the accident.) This event eventually led to the retirement of all Concorde aircraft by Air France in May 2003 and by British Airways in November of the same year.

For many of us, traumatic historical events that we live through often sear our memories of the activities of the exact moment we hear news of such events. Many folks who were alive during the time of President Kennedy's assassination or the tragedy of 9/11 remember precisely where they were and what they were doing when they heard of them. The day of the Concorde crash remains burned in my memory. Concorde's passenger numbers soon fell, however, thus eventually sealing its fate. It could not recover its glory days, and eventually, all were retired.

The Concorde's last commercial flight was from New York's JFK Airport to London's Heathrow Airport. Aboard were several show business notables and an Ohio couple who reportedly paid $60K on eBay for two tickets. (A round-trip trans-Atlantic fare was $9K then.) A large crowd of spectators greeted the plane's arrival in London, which coincided with two other final Concorde flights from Edinburgh and the Bay of Biscay. Flying at a maximum speed that was over twice as fast as the speed of sound, this marvel of modern engineering was capable of flying faster than a speeding bullet while doing so at an altitude of 60,000 ft. Concorde had been in service for 27 years, making its first commercial flight on January 21, 1976.

One particular Concorde sighting of mine took place on a beautiful starry night while flying north over the country of CHAD on the African continent at an altitude of 41,000 ft in a Learjet. We were bound for Benghazi, Libya, which served as a technical fuel stop on the way to Athens, Greece, from the Central African Republic. Monitoring HF Radio, it was tuned to Nicosia Radio. This was very late at night, so there wasn't much chatter to be heard on the frequency. Settling in for the long flight, my right seater was slumped in his seat, looking up at the stars, when he noticed red and green identification lights and a strobe flashing far above our altitude, moving at a high rate of speed.

"What the hell is that?" he asked.

On frequency, we heard: "Allo Nicky, Allo Nicky. Speed bird calling, do you read?"

This call was made to Nicosia Radio on the same frequency we were monitoring. Nicosia answered and requested an estimate for some fixes along their route. Assuming our sighting was the Concorde, I called Speed Bird, asking how their ride was and their altitude and speed, mentioning they had just passed us as we flew north at FL410.

Replying, they responded: "Allo Learjet. We are currently at FL600 at Mach 2.02. Swift and smooth, lad! A beautiful night indeed. Lovely talking with you. Enjoy your flight. Goodbye."

And with that, they were gone—an unforgettable sight.

A second encounter with the Concorde occurred at Heathrow Airport in London sometime later. After we had parked the aircraft and our passengers had departed, we noticed a Concorde taxiing for takeoff on the opposite side of the runway between us. Hoping to get an up-close look at the beast as it rotated, we walked as far out as we dared to get a better view. Suddenly, an airport vehicle appeared.

Expecting to be told to move back, the window being rolled down. A uniformed man asked if we would like a better look at the take-off of the Concorde experience.

"You betcha!" I replied.

"Come on then. Get aboard," he said.

Calling Heathrow ground control, he requested permission to drive onto the grass between the parallel runways several thousand feet from the departure end of the Concorde's runway.

"This is about where the Concorde will rotate. Please cover your ears, lads. When it passes, it's going to be quite loud. He will be in full 'afterburner,' as you Yanks call it while passing."

'LOUD' was an understatement. As the aircraft rotated at

almost the exact spot we were standing, the sound of several tornadoes with an erupting volcano thrown in roared past as the pressure wave threatened to bowl us over. It was an unbelievable experience. Unfortunately, no one thought to take a picture. It was a once-in-a-lifetime picture-taking opportunity missed, but a once-in-a-lifetime experience, nonetheless. The Concorde was an exceptional aircraft whose days were numbered, but whose record still stands witness to the ever-evolving challenges of supersonic flight.

In 2016, Richard Branson announced plans to launch a new supersonic passenger jet dubbed Concorde II. The jet is claimed to fly from London to New York in three and a half hours. The entrepreneur is working with the American startup company Boom to develop the XB-1 supersonic aircraft, set to be the "fastest civil aircraft ever made."

In September 2017, the US space agency NASA and aircraft manufacturer Lockheed Martin revealed they were also developing a supersonic aircraft that would fly across the Atlantic in three hours and be much quieter than the Concorde. In 2021, NASA released a time-lapse video of construction work on QueSST dubbed 'Son of Concorde.' According to their website, NASA will officially take delivery of the aircraft from Lockheed Martin in early 2023. I haven't yet heard if that has occurred.

Supersonic flight isn't a challenge for the future; it is being undertaken as history struggles into the mid-twentieth century and beyond. Stand by for updates.

Chapter Thirty-One
"ALARMING SILENCE"

* Glide Distance = Half the distance from an airplane to the nearest emergency landing field.

The Gimli Glider!

A double engine flameout while flying at 41,000 ft en route to Edmonton, Alberta, on July 23, 1983, Air Canada Flight 143, a Boeing 767, became the world's heaviest commercial passenger service and glider ever to take to the skies!

It was cruising at 41,000 ft over Red Lake, Ontario. The aircraft's cockpit warning system sounded, indicating a fuel pressure problem on its left side. Assuming a fuel pump had failed, the pilots turned it off since gravity should feed fuel to the aircraft's two engines. The aircraft's fuel gauges were inoperative because of an electronic fault indicated on the instrument panel and airplane logs (the pilots believed flight to be legal with this malfunction).

The flight management computer indicated that there was still sufficient fuel for the flight, but the initial fuel load had been entered as pounds instead of kilograms. A few moments later, a second fuel pressure alarm sounded for the right engine, prompting the pilots to divert to Winnipeg. The left engine failed within seconds, and they began preparing for a single-engine landing. Communicating their intentions to controllers in Winnipeg as they attempted to restart the left engine, the cockpit warning system sounded again with the 'all engines out' sound, an extended 'bong' that no one in the cockpit could recall having heard before. (It was not covered in flight simulator training.) Flying with all engines out was never expected to occur and had never been covered in training.

Seconds later, the right-side engine also stopped, the 767 lost all power, and most of the instrument panels in the cockpit went blank. In line with their planned diversion to Winnipeg, the pilots were already descending through 35,000 ft when the second engine shut down. They immediately searched their emergency checklist for the section on flying the aircraft with both engines out, only to find that no such section existed.

Captain Pearson made his best guess about the 767's glide speed, flying the aircraft at 220 knots (410 km/h; 250 mph). First Officer Maurice Quintal began to calculate whether they could reach Winnipeg. He used the altitude from one of the mechanical backup instruments. At the same time, the air traffic controllers in Winnipeg supplied the distance traveled by measuring the distance the aircraft's echo moved on their radar screens. The aircraft lost 5,000 ft (1,500 m) in 10 nautical miles (19 km; 12 mi), giving a glide ratio of approximately 12:1. Gliders that Captain Pearson was familiar with had glide ratios of 50:1/70:1.

At this point, Quintal proposed landing at the former RCAF Station Gimli, a closed air force base where he had once served as a Royal Canadian Air Force pilot. Unknown to him, part of the facility had been converted into a racetrack complex, now known as Gimli Motorsports Park. It included a road racecourse, a go-kart track, and a drag strip.

A Canadian Automobile Sport Clubs-sanctioned sports car race, hosted by the Winnipeg Sports Car Club, was underway on the Saturday of the accident. The area around the decommissioned runway was full of cars and campers, and part of the runway was used to stage the race. Without power, the pilots had to try lowering the aircraft's main landing gear via a gravity drop. The main gear locked into position, but the nose wheel failed to lock into position, which later turned out to be a blessing in disguise. When the aircraft slowed on approach to landing, the ram air turbine generated less power, rendering the aircraft increasingly challenging to control.

As the runway drew near, it became apparent that the aircraft was too high and fast, raising the danger of running off the runway before the plane could be stopped. The lack of hydraulic pressure prevented flap/slat extension, which would have, under normal landing conditions, reduced the aircraft's stall speed and increased the lift coefficient of the wings, allowing the aircraft to be slowed for a safe landing. The pilots briefly considered executing a 360-degree turn to reduce speed and altitude, but they did not have enough altitude for the maneuver. Pearson agreed to perform a forward slip to increase drag and lose altitude. This maneuver is commonly used with gliders and light aircraft to descend more quickly without increasing the already-too-fast forward speed.

With both engines dead, the plane made hardly any noise during its approach. This gave people on the ground no warning of the impromptu landing and little time to flee. As the gliding plane closed in on the decommissioned runway, the pilots noticed two boys were riding bicycles within 1,000 ft of the projected point of impact. Captain Pearson later said that the boys were so close that he could see the sheer terror on their faces as they realized a large aircraft was bearing down on them.

Two factors helped avert disaster: the failure of the front landing gear to lock into position during the gravity drop and a guardrail installed along the center of the repurposed runway to facilitate its use as a drag racetrack. Without slats extended, the aircraft was flown to the ground at a much faster rate than usual. Pearson braked hard when the wheels touched the runway, skidding and promptly blowing out two of the aircraft's tires. The unlocked nose wheel collapsed and was forced back into its well, causing the aircraft's nose to slam into, bounce off, and then scrape along the ground. This additional friction helped to slow the airplane and kept it from crashing into the crowds surrounding the runway. Pearson applied extra right brake pressure, which caused the main landing gear to straddle the guardrail, which was now dividing the strip, further slowing the plane down. The Air Canada Flight 143 came to a final stop on the ground 17 minutes after running out of fuel.

None of the 61 passengers were seriously hurt. Racers and course workers armed with fire extinguishers extinguished a minor fire in the nose area. The aircraft's nose had collapsed onto the ground, elevating its tail. Some minor injuries occurred when passengers exited the aircraft via the rear slides, which were not long enough to accommodate the increased height.

The cause of the accident was a simple mathematical error between the ground crew and the pilots. They arrived at an incorrect conversion factor of 1.77, weighing a liter of fuel in pounds. This conversion factor was provided on the refueller's paperwork and was always used for the airline's imperial-calibrated fleet.

Their calculation produced:

7682 L × 1.77 kg/L = 13597 kg

22300 kg – 13597 kg = 8703 kg

8703 kg ÷ (1.77 kg/L) = 4916 L

(1 Kilogram = 2.2 LBS)

Fuel to be transferred: instead of 22,300 kg of fuel, they had 22,300 pounds on board—10,100 kilograms, about half the amount required to reach their destination. Knowing the problems with the FQIS, Captain Pearson double-checked their calculations but was given the same incorrect conversion factor and inevitably came up with the exact erroneous figures.

The incident was caused by a series of issues, starting with a failed fuel-quantity indicator sensor (FQIS). These had high failure rates in the early 767s, and the only available replacement was also nonfunctional. The problem was logged, but later, the maintenance crew misunderstood the situation and turned off the backup FQIS. This required the fuel to be manually measured using a dipstick. The navigational computer required the fuel to be entered in kilograms. Still, an incorrect conversion from volume to mass was applied, which led the pilots and ground crew to agree that it was carrying enough fuel for the remaining trip. The aircraft was carrying only 45% of its required fuel load. The plane ran out of fuel halfway to Edmonton.

In Edmonton, maintenance staff were waiting to install a working FQIS that they borrowed from another airline. The Board of Inquiry found fault with Air Canada's procedures, training, and manuals and recommended adopting fueling procedures and other safety measures that European airlines already use. The board also recommended immediately converting all Air Canada aircraft from imperial units to metric units since a mixed fleet was more dangerous than an all-imperial or an all-metric fleet. Following Air Canada's internal investigation, Captain Pearson was demoted for six months, and First Officer Quintal was suspended for two weeks for allowing the incident to happen. Three maintenance workers were also suspended. In 1985, Pearson and Quintal were awarded the first-ever Fédération Aéronautique Internationale Diploma for Outstanding Airmanship. Several attempts by other crews who were given the same circumstances in a simulator in Vancouver resulted in crashes.

Quintal was promoted to captain in 1989. Pearson remained with Air Canada for ten years and then moved to fly for Asiana Airlines; he retired in 1995. Maurice Quintal died at 68 on September 24, 2015, in Saint-Donat, Quebec.

On 24 January 2008, the Gimli Glider, AC7067, took its final voyage from Montreal Trudeau to Tucson International Airport before retiring in the Mojave Desert.

Chapter Thirty~Two
"FLYING ON EMPTY"

The Azores Glider!

On August 24, 2001, Air Transat flight 236, an Airbus 330, departed Toronto, Canada, destined for Lisbon, Portugal. Captain Robert Piche, 48, was in command with a total flying time of 16,800 hours, of which 796 hours were in the A330. He was also an experienced glider pilot. The First Officer Dirk DeJager, 28, had 4,800 flying hours, 386 of which were in the A330. Together, they glided the plane to a successful emergency landing in the Azores, saving 306 souls.

Approximately four hours into the flight, the aircraft began leaking fuel through a fracture that had developed in a fuel line to the #2 engine. The pilots eventually noticed a low oil temperature and a high oil pressure on the #2 engine. Although these indications were an indirect result of the fuel leak, the pilots had no reason to suspect it as the cause. Captain Piche, suspecting false warnings but sharing his concern, contacted Montreal's Air

Traffic Control Center. They advised monitoring the situation. The indications of a fuel problem were becoming more evident but, as yet, unnoticed by the crew.

- The fuel on board decreased unusually, as displayed in the Fuel-On-Board (FOB) figures on the Engine Warning Display screen.

- The estimated Fuel-On-Board at the destination would have decreased, indicating a reduced fuel range.

- The full forward transfer of the fuel in the trim tank was premature. A TRIM TANK XFR annunciator light was evident for a prolonged 19 minutes, followed by a TRIM TANK XFRD indication, all premature.

Rather than referring to the appropriate checklists, the crew actioned procedures from memory, feeding fuel into an already leaking engine. The transferred fuel was lost through the fractured fuel line, leaking at a rate of approximately one gallon per second. This was caused by a higher-than-normal fuel flow through the fuel-oil heat exchanger, leading to a drop in oil temperature and a rise in oil pressure. Declaring a fuel emergency, Captain Piche decided to divert to Lajes Air Base, located on the island of Terceira in the Azores.

While still 150 nautical miles from Lajes Air Base and at 39,000 ft, the #2 engine flamed out from fuel starvation. Piche initiated a descent to 33,000 ft, the proper single-engine altitude for the aircraft's weight. Ten minutes later, a MAYDAY was transmitted to Santa Maria Oceanic air traffic control. Thirteen minutes later, and about 65 NM from Lajes Air Base, the #1 engine also flamed out. The Airbus 330 was now a glider. The deployed Ram Air Turbine provided essential electrical power to flight instruments and hydraulic power to primary flight controls. Hydraulic power was lost to the flaps and spoilers. Slats were still powered. A limited number of brake applications were available from the brake accumulators. Five minutes later, the passenger oxygen masks deployed.

Descending at 2,000 ft per minute, they calculated they had approximately 15 to 20 minutes before they would have to ditch in the ocean. Fortunately, a few minutes later, the air base was sighted. Still very high, a 360 was made, and "S" turns to dissipate excess altitude.

The aircraft touched down very hard on Rwy 33, bouncing once, then touched down again at roughly 2,800 ft from the landing threshold of the 10,000 ft runway. Maximum emergency braking was applied, stopping the aircraft after approximately 7,600 ft of landing rollout. The anti-skid was inoperative. The eight main wheels deflated, abraded, and wore themselves down to the axles. The aircraft suffered structural damage to the main landing gear from the hard touchdown, fuselage deformation, and punctures caused by debris impact from the main landing gear.

It was found that the fuel leak resulted from installing an incorrect part of the hydraulic system during an engine change. An older spare engine, which did not include a hydraulic pump, was used. A modification was made to that engine from a similar engine, an adaptation that did not maintain adequate clearance between the hydraulic and fuel lines. This lack of clearance, just millimeters, allowed chafing between the lines to rupture the fuel line, causing the leak. This modification was approved by the airline's maintenance department against the mechanic's wishes, who were involved in the process.

Conclusions:

- The flight crew did not detect a fuel problem until the FUEL ADV advisory was displayed, and a fuel imbalance was noted on the fuel ECAM page.

- The crew did not correctly evaluate the situation before taking action.

The crew did not recognize that a fuel leak existed and carried out the fuel imbalance procedure from memory, resulting in the fuel from the left tanks being fed to the leak in the right engine. Conducting the FUEL IMBALANCE procedure from memory negated the defense of the caution note in the FUEL IMBALANCE checklist. This may have caused the crew to consider taking timely action regarding the FUEL LEAK procedure. As stated, the aircraft checklist may have helped determine the problem and the correct method to follow, thus revealing the problem.

- Many other indications of a fuel leak occurred, yet the crew did not conclude that a leak existed.

- Not actioning the FUEL LEAK procedure was the key factor that led to fuel exhaustion.

The Portuguese, French, and Canadian Aviation Accident Prevention and Investigation Departments determined that crew actions in mishandling a fuel leak in the #2 engine were the primary causal factors in the accident. Air Transat was fined $250,000 for its unapproved engine modification.

Airbus Industries modified the AIRPLANE FLIGHT MANUAL. The onboard computers were upgraded to check all fuel levels against the flight plan, giving a clear warning if fuel is being expended beyond the specific fuel consumption rate of the engines. Rolls-Royce also issued a bulletin advising them of the incompatibility of the relevant engine parts. The DGCA and FAA also issued an Airworthiness Directive.

No action was taken against either pilot. They returned to a hero's welcome from the Canadian press. Captain Piche was awarded the "Superior Airmanship Award" by the Airline Pilots Association.

Chapter Thirty-Three
"THUNDER FROM THE SKY"

"A Tribute to a Dear Friend, Patriot & Hero"

The Man Who Controlled the Lightning!

Bob Vaucher was born December 3, 1918, in Mission, TX. I first met Lt. Col. Bob Vaucher (Pronounced Vooshay) when he attended a Quiet Birdman meeting at the Somerville, NJ Hangar. The date was January 2017. He was 99 years young. Introductions were made as many members had never met nor known of this amazingly spry 99-year-old's remarkable life.

Votes were taken among the members that night, and an overwhelming invitation to join the 'good fellows' ranks was extended and accepted. Col. Bob became a cherished member of the Somerville Quiet Birdman Hangar. Below is Bob blowing out the birthday cake candles as he celebrates his 100th birthday in December 2018.

I enjoyed sitting at the same table and sharing a meal with Col. Bob. Hearing I had written a book, he mentioned he would love to read it. I signed a copy for him. When I saw him next, he said he loved it and asked many questions about my career that paled in comparison. Bob was a delightful friend, an American hero, and a bonafide 'Good Fellow.'

Bob's interest and remarkable aviation career began in 1933. While still in the eighth grade, he joined 'The Flying Club of America,' which had been instituted by Gen. 'Hap' Arnold, one of a few visionaries in building America's military foundation, and to create a pool of youth with a background in aviation and technology. According to Bob, General Marshall created the Citizens Military Training Camp (CMTC) two years later. The idea was to create a pool of young individuals with military training.

His first year saw Bob as an infantryman. At Fort Bullis, TX, while on maneuvers in 1936, Bob and his company were pinned down for quite a while when aircraft flew overhead, keeping them pinned to the ground. "That's when I decided to become a pilot,"

Bob said. "Those guys in those airplanes were going back to base and their girlfriends while I'm stuck here on the ground lying in Poison Ivy."

Much later, Bob enrolled in Pan-American University to obtain the required degree for acceptance into pilot training. During his second year, he enrolled in a flight training course and, at the age of 21, earned his private pilot's certificate. The Air Corps then accepted anyone with two years of college for flight training. In April 1941, Bob completed his pilot training and was commissioned a Lieutenant in the Army Air Corps.

By this time, Hitler had already invaded Poland and annexed Czechoslovakia. The winds of war were rapidly reaching gale force. Eight months before the attack on Pearl Harbor, Bob was assigned to the Second Bomb Wing at Langley Field, VA—training to fly the B-17. Precisely, one day after the bombing of Pearl, he was told his training was over. At 23, he was now a full-fledged Army Air Corps aircraft commander. He piloted his first patrol mission in a B-18 'Bolo' medium bomber, looking for German ships and submarines off the east coast. It was just nine days after the Japanese attack on Pearl Harbor.

Aviation technology was still rapidly evolving during this time. Man had just learned to fly 38 years earlier. And now, in 1942, a new plane, the B-29, was in production. The military wanted experienced pilots to test it. The B-29 represented a significant leap forward from previous bombers. It flew faster, higher, and further, and carried a heavier bomb load. The US wanted this bomber in the war as fast as possible. However, the B-29 had many problems, including major safety issues, and needed refinement. Enter Lt. T. Robert Vaucher. The testing of the B-29 was hazardous. Bob would later say that it was more dangerous than actual bombing runs. On one test, Bob flew the plane up to 38,000 ft, testing the pressurization system. He later said he thought it was "pretty close to outer space" as he had never flown that high. An altitude that only a handful of fliers had ever been.

After this test, he received a call from General Hap Arnold, the head of the Air Force, who asked him several questions about it, congratulated him, and lauded his bravery. After the B-29 was tested on the home front, it was time for the plane and its crews to join the battle overseas.

At first, the B-29s were stationed in India, where they would begin their bombing runs toward Japan. Bob piloted twenty runs of those from India. This bombing route was a long trek over the Himalayan Mountains (The Hump), requiring a fuel stop in China. They needed to be closer. A close friend of mine whose father also flew the 'Hump' in DC-3s told him that those mountains were euphemistically referred to as the 'Aluminum Mountains' because so many wrecked aircraft dotted their slopes.

By 1945, the US had secured islands in the Pacific that would provide a better launch site to hit Japan. The entire B-29 outfit be moved to Tinian Island in the Pacific in April 1945. From there, Bob led another ten bombing missions over Japan. The bombing done by the B-29s was very effective. It destroyed many cities along with their war-producing factories. While efficient and effective, each bombing mission was still dangerous. Many planes and men were lost. The Japanese defenses hit Bob's plane when returning from the first of several firebombing raids; he flew to Kobe, Japan. 96 Japanese fighters engaged the B-29s in 128 attacks carried out by Bob's bomber wing. Two B-29s were lost and two of the airmen in the downed aircraft were captured and later executed by the Japanese.

Bob's plane was in bad shape with fuel leaking, but it was still flying. One engine was out. They were unable to make their home base at Tinian but had a couple of options. They could try to contact a US submarine and ditch the plane, hoping to be picked up. Or they could try to make an emergency landing on an island on the route back to Tinian. Iwo Jima was the island that had only just been taken from the Japanese a month before in a bloody battle led by the US Marines. In that battle, John Basilone (posthumously awarded the Medal of Honor) was killed as he got a previously stalled attack started.

Bob managed to fly the crippled plane safely to Iwo Jima. The plane, with well over 400 holes, was later junked. Out of eleven crew, only one crewman suffered a minor wound. Shrapnel from a Flak attack almost removed a portion of one finger. In an interview, Bob said that he was grateful to the Marines and John Basilone for having fought to create this emergency landing site, for it saved his and his crew's lives.

Before each bombing attack, bombers would fly over the target cities and drop leaflets announcing their intentions to bomb the city the next day, urging residents to leave the city. Kobe was no exception. "The Japanese were beaten long before the atomic bomb was dropped on Hiroshima," Bob said. On June 5 of that same year, Kobe was bombed again. Incendiaries were dropped from 530 B-29 bombers. The firebombing of Kobe with incendiary bombs under the order of Gen Curtis LeMay devastated a total of seven square miles of the city and the surrounding area.

The Japanese announced their intent to surrender on August 15, 1945. The 'Instrument of Surrender' was formally signed on the deck of the Iowa-class battleship, USS MISSOURI, BB63, on September 2, 1945. At the request of General of the Army, General

Douglas MacArthur, General Curtis LeMay was assigned the task of organizing a traditional 'Show of Force' to the vanquished enemy. General LeMay chose Lt. Col. Bob Vaucher to lead a squadron of 525 B-29s to fly over the decks of the USS MISSOURI at exactly the moment of the signing of the 'Instrument of Surrender' document by General MacArthur.

General Richard K. Sutherland witnessed the Japanese signing the 'Instrument of Surrender.'

For the signing ceremony, General MacArthur, a military historian, sought to demonstrate to the defeated side that they had made the right decision in surrendering. What greater message of defeat could be made than those 525 B-29s flying over the USS Missouri as the 'Instrument of Surrender' document was signed?

Lt. Col. Bob Vaucher was chosen to lead and command this historic flyover. On the day of the surrender, he flew the lead plane, with hundreds of other B-29s following him. He hit his mark of 9:08 am as the sky darkened with shadows of the 'aluminum overcast' of 525 B-29s.

General of the Army Douglas MacArthur signed the Instrument of Surrender on behalf of the Allied Powers. Generals Wainwright and Percival, both former prisoners of the Japanese, stand behind him.

It was a fantastic sight that accomplished its purpose. Col. Bob Vaucher was an excellent choice for this mission, as he had implemented improvements and had flown 116 combat missions—this fly-over being the 117th.

Bob flew the first and last B-29 bombing missions over Japan. Yokohama was the first, and Kobe the last, just before the Japanese capitulation. His 117 B-29 missions resulted in him accumulating 3,000 hours as a command pilot of the B-29. A few of the 'firsts' attributed to Bob:

- Piloted the first B-29 Super Fortress Heavy Bomber accepted from Boeing, delivering the aircraft to the United States Air Corps 40th Bombardment Group (VH) at Pratt, Kansas, in July 1943.

- Flew as aircraft commander on the first B-29 strategic combat mission against mainland Japan on June 15, 1944.

- Selected as mission commander to Yokohama, the largest and most destructive (8.90 sq. miles, 2,590 tons of bombs) single in-trail assembly of B-29s (454) over a target on May 29, 1945.

- Flew the longest non-stop WWII combat mission (4,030 nautical miles round-trip, 18 hrs., 50 min., India to Sumatra).

- Flying the aircraft beyond the official max. range on Aug 10, 1944.

- Introduced the first radar-equipped US Bomber (LB-30) into combat in April 1942. (The LB-30 was the British version of the B-24 Liberator.)

- Piloted the first B-29 to 38,000 ft, successfully testing bomb bay door opening speed and pressurization modifications in July 1943.

- Developed and implemented improved cruise control for the B-29, which increased bomb load by nearly 50%, resulting in fewer sorties to accomplish the same results.

- Selected as mission commander for the 'Show of Force' flyover of 525 B-29s over the Japanese surrender ceremony aboard the USS Battleship Missouri on September 2, 1945.

Bob's Military Honors:

- Two Distinguished Flying Crosses, five Air Medals, eight Battle Stars,

- Thirteen War Time Commendations and Citations.

"Arsenal of Bob is in the Command seat of the B-29 again. At the "Arsenal of Democracy."

After he rode in 'DOC' with the crew!

In 1947, Eastern Airlines called on Bob to join their ranks while seeking employment. When asked what position and aircraft he would be assigned, he was told he would be a co-pilot on a DC-3. When asked how long he would hold that position, he was told that he would be upgraded to captain in about 1952. Had this individual researched Bob's background, he would have immediately hired Bob for a management position. Eastern blew it! (My opinion.)

One day, Bob had an idea. The guns on the B-29 were operated remotely. What could he do with that technology? Utilizing the early technology of the B-29, he invented and devised a measuring system that is used worldwide today in the machine tool industry. It is called the Servo-Electric Measuring System. Bob holds the patent.

Another day, he overheard two women discussing the height disparity of the ironing board. When he spoke with the woman, he was informed that the adjustable ironing board did not exist. He quickly invented the adjustable height ironing board. Although he was denied a patent for some reason, he wasn't deterred. He manufactured and distributed these himself.

In September 2020, Bob was chosen as the Honorary Air Boss for the Arsenal of Democracy (AOD) flyover in Washington, DC. Bob participated in the planning and execution of this national tribute to the 75th anniversary of World War II. He was thrilled when he flew in the B-29 Superfortress named DOC as part of his Honorary Air Boss Duties. His eyes became misty, recognizing that his sacrifice and the sacrifice of millions more had not been forgotten.

Bob's wartime call sign or code was: "VICTOR, ABLE UNCLE CHARLIE, HOW, EASY, ROGER; CALLING ALL CHICKENS TO THE HEN HOUSE."

All chickens come home to roost eventually, as it is their destiny.

Bob answered the call and his 'Rendezvous with Destiny' when, on February 7th, 2021, he 'Went West' and I miss him!

Lt. Col. Thomas Robert (Bob) Vaucher, QB # 42401, SOM.

Chapter Thirty-Four
"THE WEIGHT OF HISTORY"

Jack Knight and Transcontinental Air Service!

In 1921, a young airmail pilot became the most famous flyer in America seven years before Charles Lindbergh made his historic solo flight across the Atlantic Ocean. His name was Jack Knight. What's that? You have never heard of Jack Knight? Let me introduce you!

The US transcontinental mail route began operating in September 1920. However, since pilots did not fly after dark, the mail was transferred to a rail car to travel during the night. A waiting plane would take the mail sacks and fly on at dawn.

Daylight navigation in the early days of airmail, before the advent of lighted beacons, was accomplished using an erratic whiskey compass, a road map, and large concrete arrows poured into the ground to point in the correct direction of travel. While reasonably large, these arrows could be easily missed in a fog or heavy rainstorm. Pilots would occasionally find themselves many miles from their programmed course. They would land at small airfields and then proceed, once reoriented, to their original course.

Jack Knight

James H. "Jack" Knight was a twenty-eight-year-old aviator who, in February 1921, was part of an airmail team that flew 2,629 miles across the United States to show that the airmail service was faster than the railroads.

Airmail was in its infancy in 1921. It took 78 hours to fly mail across the US. When Warren G. Harding became the 29th President of the United States in March 1921, he determined that using aircraft was too expensive. He was hell-bent on shutting down the Airmail service in favor of opting for the more reliable railroads in its place. The railroads would take 108 hours to deliver mail coast to coast and would be considerably cheaper. The President vowed to veto any proposed further funding for the service.

If that happened, Jack Knight and his fellow pilots would be out of a job. Jack's career was in jeopardy. Postmaster General Burleson and his chief of Airmail Service set out to devise a plan to guarantee mail delivery in half the time customarily accepted, to convince President Harding of the viability of continuing airmail service. There was only one way to change the president's mind: Fly the mail coast to coast in 36 hours. The government could not refuse that.

Airmail pilots at the time virtually flew by the seat of their pants. Their instrument panel included only a magnetic compass for navigation, which oscillated from north to south in rough weather. They also flew dangerously low in bad weather, skimming rivers, railroad tracks (IFR—I follow railroads), and towns at treetop level to see where they were going. Finding familiar landmarks at night would be difficult in open cockpits, which posed a significant challenge. To do so, ground fires would be lit along the way. Night watchmen would light fires in oil drums to guide the pilots on the transcontinental route.

On February 22nd, two mail planes left Hazlehurst Field on Long Island, New York, heading west, while two other aircraft left Crissy Field on San Francisco's Presidio, flying east. Relay planes waited at the regularly scheduled stops in between. At 10 PM, after multiple eastbound legs, the mail was handed off to Jack Knight, who was waiting at North Platte, Neb., to continue his eastbound leg. He was to fly the North Platte to Omaha on the relay leg. Through the frosty night, he could see the signal fires. "I felt like I had a thousand friends on the ground. Lexington, Kearney, Grand Island, Columbus, and Fremont slipped by with warm glows of well-wishers below my plane's wings. Then, I saw Omaha," he stated about that first leg.

Arriving in Omaha during a snowstorm, Jack was informed that several relay pilots were unable to fly due to being snowed in. He was told that he was the only eastbound pilot left flying. After warming himself, he continued the flight despite the threatening storm and the fact that he had never flown east of Omaha. At 2 AM, he departed for Des Moines, the next leg of the flight. As word spread, he navigated again by fires lit by night watchmen and now by postal employees, farmers, and well-wishers.

Unable to land in Des Moines due to the snowstorm, Jack flew an additional 120 miles to Iowa City, freezing and numb from the cold. He stopped just long enough to warm himself, refuel, and eat a ham sandwich before again taking to the foreboding air en route to Chicago at 6:30 AM. Flying a further 200 miles, he landed in Chicago at 8:40 AM. His all-night flight covered 830 miles and lasted just short of 11 hours in the air, while navigating by ground fires, a basic compass, and a small, torn road map.

No airmail pilot had ever flown the mail at night before. Even though freezing in his open-cockpit aircraft and flying almost blind through a blizzard, Jack recognized that failure was not an option. He not only made history but he was also awarded hero status. The day's headlines were "Jack Knight's Night Flight," regaling his frozen flight through a blizzard to get the mail through, and "The Man That Saved The Night Airmail," making him the most famous flyer of the pre-Lindbergh era.

Although Knight was a hero, the feat was a team victory as two other pilots continued to New York, making the remaining daytime flight in record time. Altogether, seven pilots had taken part in the transcontinental flight, which took 33 hours and 20 minutes to complete, covering 2,629 miles.

Completing the flight in less than 36 hours impressed President Harding and his staff immensely. Harding agreed to fund the US Transcontinental Airmail Service into the future. Equally impressed by the feat and wide public acclaim, Congress finally appropriated the funds needed for the beleaguered Airmail Service. Appropriations were soon apportioned for a lighted Beacon system to support the fledgling air service during later harrowing night flights.

1921 Postage Stamp Beacon

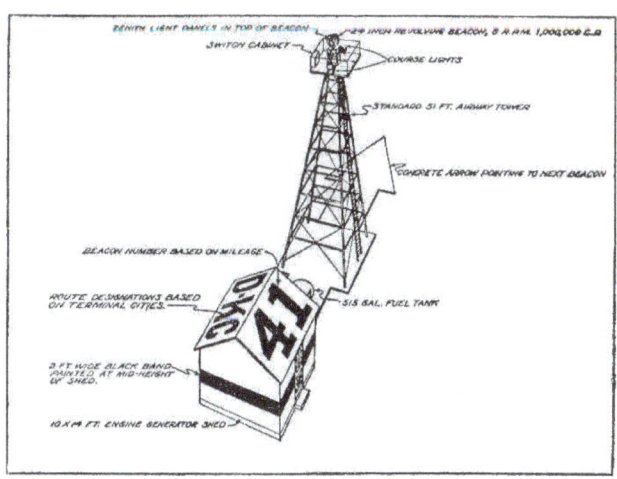

Beacon Shed

The remnants of a concrete Arrow

Was Jack an early member of the QBs? The Quiet Birdmen was founded in 1921 when Jack saved the US airmail service. This is an interesting question that QB historians should ponder. Jack went west in February 1945.

Chapter Thirty~Five
"YE ANCIENT AND SECRET SOCIETY OF FLYING BIRDMEN"

Generaloberst Udet circa 1941

The Nazi Luftwaffe General!

In November 1919, while in France, a group of American World War I aviators started a drinking club and called themselves 'The American Flying Club.' After the Armistice of November 1918, the club reconvened in New York City. In January 1921. A subset of that group, six original aviators, began meeting regularly on Monday nights at an Italian restaurant in Greenwich Village called Marta's.

Harold Hersey, the editor of *Aces High* magazine, ironically called the group the 'Quiet Birdmen,' an oxymoron since they were boisterous. Soon, the noisy group, bothering other patrons, was barred from holding their meetings at Marta's. Subsequent meetings were held at different locations each time, often in a restaurant. It was not until 1938 that a permanent meeting location was established. It was in a building owned by the Architectural League of New York.

Membership in those early days was one dollar and lasted until death. This was the official birth of Ye Ancient and Secret Order of Quiet Birdmen. A blue shield with the letters "QB" in silver, flanked by silver wings, became the club's emblem, worn by many proud goodfellows ever since.

Many of our twentieth-century aviation heroes were QB members. We all know who they were. Charles Lindbergh and Jimmy Doolittle are just two of the more famous members. However, few know the name of the foreigner and famous WWI flying ace credited with 62 confirmed kills, and who later gained admittance to the Quiet Birdmen. Eddie Rickenbacker comes to mind, but a foreigner. (Eddie Rickenbacker, an American WWI flying ace, was undoubtedly an early QB member; however, he was credited with only twenty-six confirmed kills.)

Ernst Udet was the highest-scoring German fighter pilot to survive that war and the second most famous German flyer after Baron Manfred von Richthofen, 'The Red Baron' of Flying Circus fame and Ernst's commander. (The Red Baron, the highest-scoring German ace with eighty kills, did not survive the war.)

A Young Ernst Udet, (circa 1917) and Captain Eddie Rickenbacker

Udet became a squadron commander under Richthofen and later under Hermann Goering, was the only WWI German ace admitted to the Quiet Birdman group and was admitted under the guidelines of the 'Quiet Birdman Document.' This fascinating piece of aviation history is not well known even by many of today's QB members. This QB document was a secret agreement made in the 1930s between an American and a German aviator. Its purpose was to foster goodwill and friendship between former World War I combatants despite their previous roles as adversaries. The key players in this document were Ernst Udet, the famous German fighter pilot of WWI fame, and Eddie Rickenbacker. Udet became a Quiet Birdman, enjoying Eddie's friendship.

Due to its secretive nature, the exact details of the QB document remain undisclosed. However, it is believed that the agreement focused on promoting peace, understanding, and camaraderie among aviators. The QB gatherings provided a platform for these former adversaries to socialize and share their passion for aviation. Udet's involvement in the QBs exemplifies how aviation transcends national boundaries. Despite their wartime roles, his friendship extended to American aviators, such as Charles Lindbergh. This historic and secret document serves as a testament to the power of shared interests in bridging gaps between nations.

That QB document symbolizes an extraordinary chapter in aviation history—when former adversaries came together under the banner of flight, leaving behind past conflicts.

Udet spent the inter-war years of the 1920s and early 1930s as a stunt pilot, international barnstormer, playboy, and light aircraft manufacturer, building an aircraft he called the U2. During those intra-war years, he gained fame and international acclaim, performing dangerous aerial stunts that had never been seen or attempted. He flew for the movies and airshows by flying under bridges and performing loops only a few feet above the ground. One stunt only Udet performed was successive loops, with the last completed after securing the engine in mid-air and landing the aircraft in a slip. (Shades of Bob Hoover).

Another of his unique and dangerous stunts was diving on a runway and, while on a steep left bank, snagging a white handkerchief with the low wing tip as he climbed away. (This stunt can be seen on a YouTube Video). In early 1933, Udet's stunt pilot work in films took him to California, where he met Carl Laemmle, the founder and head of Universal Studios. While filming SOS Eisenberg, a US-German coproduction, Udet was introduced to the Curtiss Hawk aircraft. (The Navy later renamed the Curtiss Goshawk dive bomber.) Udet fell in love with its agile performance and 700+ horsepower engine.

The Curtis Hawk

When Udet returned to Germany, the Nazi Party was in its infancy. His old WWI fighter pilot friend and former commander, Herman Goering, was now the head of the new Luftwaffe, which was illegal under the terms of the Versailles Treaty. Hitler set out to build the greatest Luftwaffe ever conceived and use it for world domination.

Goering recognized the propaganda value of the second most famous German flyer, asking Udet several times to join the Nazi party. Udet repeatedly refused until Goering purchased two Curtiss Hawk aircraft as a gift to him. Udet couldn't refuse the offer and sold his soul to the devil to become a party member. Always an alcohol lover, he had a bar built and installed in his favorite. 'Hawk.' He would often fly while sipping cognac.

One day, while demonstrating the flight qualities of the

Ernst's custom-designed Curtis Bar

Curtiss Hawk, Udet dove the aircraft vertically during a demonstration flight, which eventually led to the development of the JU-88 Stuka dive bomber. It is also said that he was responsible for the "Jericho Trumpet" siren, which struck terror in the hearts of all who heard its shrill shriek as the aircraft dove upon them; however, this has never been substantiated. Udet, known primarily for his work as a stunt pilot and his playboy-like behavior, was soon appointed the director of Research and Development and rapidly rose through the ranks under the auspices of Goering. He was promoted to General-Oberst (Colonel-General) of the Luftwaffe and later installed as the head of Luftwaffe Procurement, a position Udet felt grossly and inadequately qualified for.

With the advent of Operation Barbarossa and the invasion of the Soviet Union in June of 1941, Udet became even sadder. Hearing rumors of atrocities and mass executions of Soviet POWs and Soviet Jews, he could not bring himself to believe them. For several months, he attempted to speak with Hitler, Goering, and several high-ranking generals regarding Nazi atrocities as well as the futility of attacking the Soviet Union. He was aware he was becoming a marked man., recognizing early on that the war was lost, he furtively tried to come to terms with his part in it, resorting to the taking of amphetamines and other drugs to help him cope.

Never an ardent Nazi believer, he eventually came increasingly to the realization the devil now owned his soul. The price: A Curtis Hawk. A heavy price paid in despondency. In desperation, he would mention to friends and associates that he was considering taking his own life. No one believed him. On November 17, 1941, he called his lady friend Inge Bieyle to say goodbye. He took his life by shooting himself in the head. According to Udet's biography, *The Fall of an Eagle*, he wrote a suicide note in red pencil on his bedstead saying: "Iron One, (Goring) you are responsible for my death!"

In 1975, *The Great Waldo Pepper*, starring Robert Redford, was released. It was written, produced, and directed by George Roy Hill, a pilot. The Austrian actor Bo Brundin, who played Ernst Kessler, was based on Ernst Udet's real life. (*Waldo Pepper* had been on Netflix until recently.)

Ernst Udet was one of the greatest aviators of his time. He was a tragic figure, a tragic time, and a tragic ending. He was a QB for the ages!

Chapter Thirty-Six
"EDDIE RICKENBACKER"

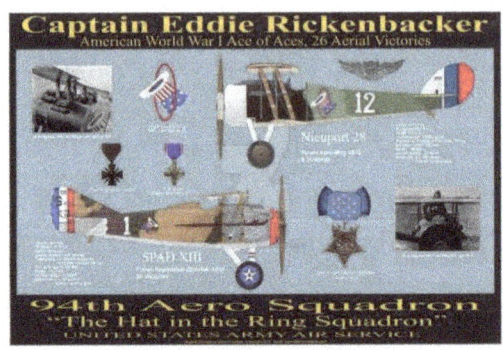

A Hero for the Ages: "The Making of a Man!" (Part One)

Edward Vernon Richenbacher was born on October 8, 1890, in Columbus, Ohio. He was the third of eight children who would become one of the most celebrated Americans of the twentieth century. However, he first had to survive his very early years.

At the age of four, Eddie was struck by a horse-drawn streetcar. Suffering only mild injuries, his good fortune was soon tested once more when he tumbled down a well, knocking himself out. He later slipped from a tree, slicing his chin, which left a lifelong scar. He was very nearly killed when his foot was caught in some railroad tracks, watching in horror as a steam engine approached. Fortunately, he was freed by his brother just in the nick of time. At eight, while racing down a hill, his out-of-control car flipped on top of him, slashing his leg to the bone. At the age of five, he was a seasoned smoker. These were just a few tribulations he would endure on his way to adulthood.

The most serious of these was to begin at the age of thirteen with the death of his father. His life changed drastically. "The day after my father's funeral, I didn't go to school—I went to work!" Quitting school the next day before finishing the seventh grade, he was off to work supporting his mother and his seven siblings, promising his mother, who was crying at the loss of her husband. "Mother, I will never make you cry."

Within hours, he made $3.50 weekly at the Federal Glass Company, walking four miles daily to and from work. Handing his mother his first paycheck was the "proudest moment of my life," he would later claim. Fearing folks would discover he could not read or write as well as them, he masked his shortcomings by charging into matters before anyone could guess the truth.

One day, noticing a crowd in downtown Columbus, he came upon a salesman selling and demonstrating a Ford two-passenger automobile, the first of its kind in Columbus. Spotting Eddie in the crowd and anxious to keep the attention on this new contraption, he said: "Hey kid, you want a ride? Hop in, and we will go around the block."

Eddie was electrified. "That thrill would remain vivid all the rest of my life. It directly influenced the course I would follow for many years," he later stated.

Cars became Eddie's passion. Lee Frayer, the owner of the Buckeye Motor Company, soon noticed his repairs of bicycles and carriages. He asked Eddie to accompany him to the 1906 Vanderbilt Cup Races as his riding mechanic, which began a long association.

In 1909, while watching a train rumble along the tracks, one of the wheels kicked a red-hot cinder into Eddie's right eye. Removed later, it left a permanent blind spot, which he diligently kept hidden from others so he could continue racing.

In 1911, Lee Frayer asked Eddie to become his relief driver in the first Indianapolis 500. They finished eighth. Eddie's racing reputation and fame grew from there. Soon, he was pictured in publications and was being recognized daily. His motto then was, "Get out in front and drive like hell," which he did with relish. The newspapers dubbed him "the Baron," or "the Speedy Swiss," and "the fastest thing on wheels."

Eddie would experience several more crashes while racing but always escaped with minor bruises and scrapes. He was convinced he was living a charmed life. Constantly taunting the "Grim Reaper," he believed in his invulnerability to death. "It came to me that I could control that machine with my mind, hold it together, and if it finally collapsed, I could run it with my mind. It was a feeling of mastery, of supreme confidence." He added, "If you think disaster, you will get it. Brood about death, and you will hasten your demise. Think positively and masterfully, with confidence and faith, and life will be more secure, more fraught with action, richer in achievement and experience."

His racing days brought fame, money, and the adoration of his fans. "That was the golden period of my life," he would later write. Soon, a more imposing test—flight would quickly command his attention.

Traveling to California in 1916 to participate in a series of West Coast races, he saw a single aircraft in a field just off the road as he drove by. Never having seen an airplane up close, he stopped to examine it. Noticing him looking at the aircraft, a man approached, introducing himself as Glen Martin, the designer and builder of the aircraft; he recognized Eddie from newspaper clippings and asked if he would like a ride. Eddie, afraid of heights, accepted the invitation despite those fears. Hopping into the front seat for a thirty-minute ride above the California countryside, he was again electrified. Offered an opportunity to take the controls, Eddie put the aircraft into twists and turns. He was hooked! His future was now in the air rather than auto racing.

Within the year, the US became embroiled in the European war. (In 1914, as war broke out in Europe, Eddie changed the spelling of his last name, "Rickenbacher," to Rickenbacker, removing the "H," hoping it would sound more American lest anyone think he was German.) He was now twenty-seven. Volunteering for the fledgling air service, he was turned down out of hand. "You are too old and don't have a college degree," he was told.

However, his skill as a racer was not unnoticed, and in 1917, he was sworn in as an Army sergeant. Shipped overseas, he was selected as a chauffeur for many high-ranking officers. As luck would have it, one day, he was assigned to drive Colonel William "Billy" Mitchell, a resolute advocate of air power. This association with Col. Mitchell allowed Eddie to express his feelings about the air service and his desire to become a part of the growing air arm of the Army. He was unsure the colonel could help him realize his dream. However, one day, as he strolled along the Champs-Élysées in Paris, looking longingly toward the sky, he met an Army captain in the Army's aviation section. His name was James

E. Miller, a huge fan of Eddie's. Captain Miller commanded a flying school in Issoudun, near Tours, France. Eddie was offered a post upon completing and passing the required physical. With the help of a sympathetic doctor who ignored his age and eye injury, Eddie was assigned his new post as an engineering officer.

Rickenbacker received his commission as a first lieutenant in the Army Signal Corps and left for Issoudun. In March 1919, he received orders to join the 94th Aero Squadron, later known as

"The Hat In The Ring"— a unit of American fliers formed in Texas the previous August. They joined the front in April that year, assisting the French in the attempted rout of German fighters. They were flying outdated French NIEUPORT 28 aircraft, badly outclassed by the German fighters. Pilots feared for their lives, not so much from the "Huns" as from the plane, which tended to shed fabric from the wings during steep dives and the frequently jamming guns. German bullets not only ignited the exposed fuel tanks but would often set them afire, as the cotton fabric had been treated with a highly explosive fluid concoction for tightening. As the aircraft burst into flame, the pilot was left with a hideous choice— death by fire or leap from the burning aircraft. Pilots were not equipped with parachutes. The military "brass" of the day felt their use cowardly, making it more likely that pilots would abandon an aircraft they might otherwise fly back to base. Rickenbacker was furious with that decision. "Death by burning was the death most dreaded. I find it criminal for our higher command to withhold parachutes from us," he would state.

Eddie was not deeply religious but never went anywhere without his Catholic crucifix—safely inserted in a leather case— resting in his pocket. It was a gift from the ten-year-old daughter of a racing fan, presented to him just before he left for the war. "If you keep it with you at all times, you will never be harmed," she told him.

By the end of 1918, and only one month into his tenure, Eddie had scored his fifth kill. "Rickenbacker Gets Fifth Hun Plane" and "Daredevil Racer Is New Ace," proclaimed national newspapers. He impressed his superior officers so much that he was chosen when an opening occurred for a new commanding officer of the 94th. He had cheated death many more times on his way to a total of twenty-six confirmed kills, earning him the French Croix de Guerre and the Medal of Honor. He had flown three hundred combat hours, more than any other American aviator, and had survived 134 encounters, flying the NIEUPORT 28 and the French SPAD XIII.

On November 11, 1918, Germany agreed to a ceasefire. Eddie's record stood until WWII, when Major Richard Ira Bong downed 40 confirmed enemy aircraft as a fighter pilot, earning him the Medal of Honor.

Eddie returned to the USA and was feted, admired, wined, and dined everywhere. President William Howard Taft and Secretary of War Newton D. Baker proclaimed him, "One of the truest knights our country has ever known." The LA Times called him the "Beloved American ace of aces." Douglas Fairbanks honored Eddie with a lavish luncheon at his Beverly Hills home. The guest list included the comic actor of his day, Charlie Chaplin. His notoriety provided many opportunities to strike it rich, but he knew the charlatans who preyed on many other war heroes and refused their offers of riches. He allowed the publication of a memoir written by a ghostwriter titled "" to enhance his finances.

His luck almost ran out in 1920. As a passenger in an aircraft from Omaha, NE, the plane he was riding hit a ditch at the end of the airfield, bounced over a road, and smashed into a house. A two-by-four plank of wood punctured the side of the aircraft, missing his head by inches. Once again, he cheated the "Grim Reaper." This was just another of the close calls he would have throughout his life. He truly believed he was charmed, attributing no small amount of luck to the crucifix from that little girl of long ago.

1922 was a big year for Eddie. He was married to the lovely Adelaide Frost. Later that year, along with three other automobile executives, he started the "Rickenbacker Motor Company." This was just before the Depression, and even though the automobile was ahead of its time in new automotive innovations, it would soon fail. Eddie returned to the air, setting new cross-country flying records, which brought him additional finances. He raised $250,000 to pay off his debts and an extra $700,000 to purchase the Indianapolis Speedway, the track that launched his racing career. He took control of the track on November 1, 1927. He ordered several significant improvements and arranged for the first radio coverage of the annual Indianapolis 500 Memorial Day race. The track was closed and neglected during the war, falling into neglect and disrepair. As the war ended, the revival of the "500" appeared unlikely and in danger of being demolished in favor of development.

(Desperate to save the track where he had so many victories and memories, Eddie sold the track in 1945 to Tony Hulman. The Hulman family retained ownership until 2019 when the Penske Corporation, purchased it.)

Rickenbacker's outlook brightened further when, in 1935, he took the helm of Eastern Airlines, which was beleaguered with financial woes. He modernized a seriously outdated fleet, adding new routes and increasing wages for better productivity. Flying 200,000 miles a year, poking his nose into every airplane, ticket office, hangar, and repair shop, he posted "Captain Eddie Says" wall posters of his many famous sayings wherever he could find space. His brusque, sometimes irascible personality frequently annoyed others, but he would not be swayed once he outlined a path to success. The result: Eastern Airlines became the most profitable airline in the United States.

By the late 1930s, Eddie was still flying regularly on frequent trips to inspect factories and hangars nationwide. His seemingly charmed life almost ended on one of those routine flights. On a routine night flight from New York's LaGuardia Field to Atlanta on February 26, 1941, he was among thirteen passengers all boarding a Douglas DST called the Mexican Flyer. Pilot James A. Perry Jr., age twenty-nine, and Luther E. Thomas, age thirty-one, prepared for takeoff. Perry's inexperience—he had captained Eastern planes for only a year—bothered Rickenbacker, whose unease paled compared to Perry's discomfort with the nation's most celebrated aviator and his irascible boss looking over his shoulder.

Lifting off at 9:05 pm, the weather reports cautioned against low cloud cover and possible heavy rains closing in on the Atlanta area. Approaching Stone Mountain, eighteen miles northeast of Atlanta, Perry contacted the Atlanta tower, which notified him that the ceiling was now 300 feet at the landing minimum height. He continued his descent. The tower further advised that two Delta aircraft had missed the approach while another had landed safely. Dropping into the thick overcast, things progressed rapidly from there. Rather than turning south toward the airfield, Perry inexplicably flew westward, flying over the town of local police chief O.L. Roberts, who later said it seemed headed for a sparsely settled area with poor roads. Visibility was reported at one mile or less as the aircraft droned on, encountering rain that turned into sleet. Dropping to 500 and 300 ft, hoping to see the airfield, their time aloft was diminishing rapidly.

Rickenbacker had just put away some paperwork when he noticed the left wing dropping.

He felt the wing hit against something, which he later learned was the tops of trees, flipping the left wing up. The cabin lights extinguished. He recognized what was happening and knew the best place to be in a crashing aircraft was at the plane's rear.

He jumped from his seat and rushed to the back. The aircraft began to disintegrate before he could reach the rear of the cabin. The collision ripped the right wing from the fuselage, sending the plane into a wild somersault and knocking it directly toward other trees and into the forest south of Atlanta near the small town of Morrow, GA. The noise awakened residents in the area, wondering what it could have been. The impact crushed the cockpit, the fuselage rested inverted with its roof buried in the earth. Rickenbacker and the other passengers were thrust against the seats, armrests, and the floor. The plane, according to Rickenbacker, twisted "like a paper bag" and broke in two with him lying on the floor between the cockpit and cabin compartments. The darkness masked a nightmarish scene!

Chapter Thirty-Seven
"EDDIE RICKENBACKER"

Another Charm in the Life! (Part Two)

Rickenbacker's nighttime flight from New York's LaGuardia field to Atlanta would end in a forest south of Atlanta near the small town of Morrow, GA. The plane was last seen flying in and out of a very low overcast, estimated by the chief of police to be approximately 300 feet, possibly lower. There is a term often heard among pilots called "Scud Running." When commonly used, however, the term usually refers to darting below an overcast sky in low visibility while still in sight of the ground. What was observed that night was an aberration of the term.

Aircraft debris was scattered over almost two hundred yards, lying among downed tree branches and churned-up earth. Of the eight survivors, Rickenbacker was the most seriously injured. His left hip was fractured from the impact of hitting the terrain, which smacked him against an armrest. He experienced excruciating pain from multiple cracked bones, including his ankle, left elbow, nose, and several ribs. A gruesome slash oozed blood above his left eye, and his shattered left hip socket and pelvis shot waves of pain throughout his body. Had he not left his seat when he did, he would have been among the dead.

Held in place by debris tossed about by the impact and covered in his blood, he was becoming soaked from the gasoline dripping from a fuel tank. Afraid of dying in an explosion, he tried, with terrible waves of pain washing over him, to extricate himself from the tangled mess. He soon discovered that he was tightly encased in the wreckage. To make matters worse, he was being pelted by freezing rain. Not giving up, he forced himself upward a few inches just as a jagged piece of aluminum directly above sliced into his face and popped his left eyeball from its socket, leaving it resting on his cheek. Continuing his effort to extricate himself despite his many injuries, it nonetheless proved futile. Slumping back, he heard the sound and felt the pain as more ribs broke. He would later say it sounded like "Popcorn popping." Accepting he was trapped in the wreckage, he had little choice but to lie in his pain and hope for rescue. Then he realized a few survivors outside the wreckage must have been thrown clear.

"Let's build a fire to ward off the cold," one said.

"No, no, no, we are surrounded by leaking fuel. We will be blown up. Stop! For God's sake, do not light a match!" Eddie shouted! He was later heard to apologizing to the survivors on behalf of Eastern Airlines for the crash, as reported by one of the survivors.

Some of the surviving passengers tried to find help. One wandered around until he encountered a dog, which led him to a home belonging to a farmer, who took him to a nearby phone.

Unaware of the drama, and after the plane was reported well overdue, Eastern Airlines officials notified local ambulance and law enforcement services and Eastern airport mechanics and workers, launching a search in the Morrow and Jonesboro area. This was after speaking with the sheriff, who had last seen the aircraft. They searched in the downpour for more than six hours, slipping and sliding in the Georgia red clay, coming within 300 yards of the wreckage without spotting it due to thick vegetation and fog.

It was near dawn when the wreckage was finally stumbled upon. Bodies of the dead and injured were strewn about grotesquely as the rescuers doubted anyone could have survived the carnage they were witnessing. Deep ravines made it impossible for vehicles to approach the crash site. Thinking all were dead except for the lone survivor who made the initial call for help, they were shocked when they spotted Rickenbacker lying helpless and bloody with one of the victims draped over his feet. Broken bones protruded from his skin, with his left eye dangling gruesomely down his cheek. The sight caused several of the rescuers to turn away and vomit. Some were certain the national hero was dead. A doctor at the scene, after inspecting him, concluded that while his chances of survival were slim, "He still breathes. There is some life."

Because of the terrain, he needed to be stretchered, feeling each jolt of searing pain, only once saying, "Easy boys, don't drop me," en route to the waiting ambulance.

At the hospital, a Catholic Chaplain was called in to administer "Last Rites" as he had been given up for dead by the attending physicians. Eddie summoned enough strength to object, saying he was a "God damned Protestant like most people." A Baptist pastor was summoned shortly after to console Eddie in what was assumed to be his last moments. He told the pastor, "I am bruised but not broken in my spirit."

At that moment, the hospital's chief surgeon, Dr. Floyd W. McRae, strode in. Nurses held Eddie down on a surgical table as the doctor pushed his eye back into its socket and sewed shut the wound to the eyelid. Eddie cursed and threatened McRae. This was done without an anesthetic as it might have weakened the eye muscles, thus complicating the procedure. The doctor out-cussed his patient and ordered him to be quiet. No further objection was heard from Eddie as other surgeons wrapped him in a body cast head to toe, save for one arm.

The next ten days were a continuous battle to keep Eddie alive. With his wife at his side, several blood transfusions were administered. After several weeks, he seemed to rally, making light of his grim situation, apologizing for interrupting her work, saying, "I guess you will have to shoot me to get rid of me."

More plasma was administered as, Eddie seemed to be slipping away, taking a turn for the worse. His hip was finally reset. He would often hallucinate and thrash about in pain. He would later say that he felt as if he were standing at the gates of heaven, experiencing his final moments. "Dying is the sweetest, tenderest, most sensuous sensation I have ever experienced. Death comes disguised as a sympathetic friend. All was serene; all was calm; how wonderful it would be to float out of this world. It is easy to die. You have to fight to live.

I have fought death many times."

Anger would well up when he heard a radio broadcast from Walter Winchell, a national newspaper columnist who also hosted a radio show, announce that Eddie Rickenbaker was dying. Becoming irate at that statement, he hurled a water pitcher at the offending radio, smashing it to bits. "The radio flew apart, and Winchell's voice stopped," said Rickenbacker. "Then, I got well."

Not many weeks later, Eddie was released on crutches, happy to be going home.

Eight people and three crew members perished in that crash. A subsequent investigation determined that the pilot and co-pilot failed to properly adjust their altimeters to the airfield's barometric pressure reading, causing the plane to approach the fog at a dangerously low altitude.

Eddie never really fully recovered from the plane crash. However, his popularity peaked to rival his 1919 return to the United States. Charles Lindbergh waned in public favor during the 1930s with his uncomfortable flattery of Adolf Hitler. Eddie's fame soared; a plane crash was not going to slow him down. Returning to work at Eastern Airlines, he divided his time between the company and the nation. He was heard saying, "The more mishaps with death I faced, and the more reasons I found for not fearing him."

The crash and his survival were just another example of why Eddie genuinely believed he was living a charmed life. He felt the survival of the crash, as well as death-defying dogfights and several serious car crashes, tested him for some great purpose and opportunity that might yet come. He was spot on! The surprise bombing of Pearl Harbor on December 7, 1941, would once again call upon that impression, testing Eddie as never before!

Eddie recovering from his airplane crash of 1941.

Chapter Thirty-Eight
"WHO THE GODS WOULD DESTROY"

Part Three

H e was too old now to jump into a fighter and duel with the Japanese, but he was not too old to aid the government. His valuable reputation and aviation knowledge had accumulated through the years. General Henry H. "Hap" Arnold felt the same way. Summoned for a meeting in March of 1942 with General Arnold, the WWI ace was asked if he would be interested in boosting morale among aviation units since Pearl Harbor. "I am told they are indifferent, that they haven't got the punch they need to do the job they're being prepared for," he explained.

"I want you to go out and talk to these boys, inspire them, put some fire in them." Arnold knew Eddie's legendary status among airmen would be welcome at every base.

Eddie accepted immediately, visiting forty-one bases and traveling 15,000 miles in thirty-two days. His message emphasized teamwork, ground preparation, and, most importantly, understanding the intricacies of their aircraft and enemies. "I flew into combat with only two machine guns, a less potent engine, and no parachute. You are entering combat with a massive advantage over our 1918 squadron in training and equipment. One of your fighters has more firepower than our whole squadron had. It was gruelling!"

Even though he had seemingly recovered from the Atlanta crash, he still suffered pain that would stay with him to the end of his life.

In September of 1943, Secretary Stimson asked Eddie to deliver a secret message to General Douglas MacArthur, commander of the US Army forces in the Far East. The message had been so sensitive that Stimson asked him to memorize the dispatch before leaving the secretary's office. Neither Eddie nor MacArthur ever revealed the contents of the message. The later post-war consensus was a stern rebuke of the general for his harsh criticism of President Franklin D. Roosevelt and the top military leaders of the time, who prioritized the European war over the Pacific conflict. Rickenbacker was the perfect messenger to deliver the rebuke.

In October, Eddie left for Hawaii, changing military aircraft, then on to Brisbane, Australia, with a first stop at Canton Island, the northernmost part of the Phoenix Islands group. He would be accompanied by his friend Colonel Hans Christian Adamson, his aide, who had been granted permission to tag along by Secretary Stimson.

Colonel Adamson's friend had recently married the movie star Rosalind Russell. Russell, a devout Catholic, knowing her husband's friend to be an agnostic and his impending trip overseas with Rickenbacker, gave him the medal of St. Joseph of

Cupertino, the seventeenth-century patron saint of aviators. Protesting that he was not of her faith and dubious of all others, he consented, placing it into his pocket where it would reside all but forgotten through the coming months. Ms. Russell asked that he keep it with him as she felt it would protect him. Her remarks would prove prescient!

Landing in Hawaii on the first leg of his trip, Colonel Adamson and Eddie were introduced to his crew for the next several legs to Brisbane, Australia. They were to fly in a Boeing B-17, nicknamed "The Swooze," piloted by twenty-seven-year-old Captain William T. Cherry Jr. The co-pilot for the mission was Second Lieutenant James C. Whittaker. Lt. Whittaker, an avowed atheist and Captain Cherry often flew with one another. Whittaker later said, "As co-pilot, I have flown with Bill Cherry and have never had a better partner." He is calm in crisis, stoical in adversity, and possesses a welcome drawing humor."

Rickenbacker was, however, unimpressed with the crew. He liked that Captain Cherry had been a co-pilot for American Airlines before the war and had held that position for several years. Still, he wondered, "Why wasn't he upgraded to captain after so many years as a co-pilot?"

Eddie's unease spiked with a glance at Cherry, who looked nothing like the crisp military aviator he expected. He discovered "that my pilot was a Texan with a goatee and high-heeled cowboy boots. There wasn't much for me to do but get on board."

On October 20, 1942, they climbed aboard a well-worn Boeing B-17 that had been converted into a transport plane in Hawaii. The crew included Captain William Cherry Jr. of Abilene, Texas, and pilot Lieutenant James Whittaker of Burlingame, California, as co-pilot. Other members of the crew were Lieutenant John De Angelis of Nesquehoning, PA., navigator (The navigator, twenty-four-year-old Second Lieutenant De Angelis, had many transpacific flights, which pleased Eddie. He felt that co-pilot Whittaker was too old.) Private John Bartek of Freehold, NJ, an engineer, and Sergeant James Reynolds of Fort Jones, Calif., were the radio operators. Also along was Staff Sgt. Alexander Kaczmarczyk from Torrington, Conn., was an enlisted airman returning to his outfit in Australia after recovering from a lengthy illness. The plane was also loaded with many bags of high-priority mail and secret documents.

Engine run-up and mag checks were completed, and takeoff clearance was requested. Captain Cherry opened the throttles a moment later, and the aircraft began its takeoff roll. The takeoff on the 20th had to be aborted due to a broken hydraulic line. The nose wheel collapsed during the abort. All onboard, plus luggage, mail bags, and navigation equipment, were transferred to another B-17. The mission was classified as secret, so everything was transferred in extreme haste into a different B-17.

During the previously aborted takeoff, the navigator's sextant (Octant) had been thrown about the navigator's forward compartment when the nose wheel collapsed. (De Angelis was refused the time to check the calibration of the sensitive instrument.)

They finally took off at 1:30 am on October 21, bound for island 'X' (so designated for security reasons: Canton Island), about 1,800 miles to the southwest. Captain Cherry throttled back an hour before the estimated arrival time, slowly descended to about 1,000 feet, and began looking for Canton Island. It never came into view. Thinking they had overshot their mark, Cherry and De Angelis made a 180-degree correction and started looking for their destination from the opposite direction. Again, they saw nothing but the ocean.

Reynolds kept in constant contact with personnel at Canton. He requested a bearing, but the island did not have the equipment to provide one. Next, he contacted another island, known as "Y," for assistance and was told to circle at 5,000 feet for 30 minutes and keep sending continuous radio signals.

In the end, however, all "Y" could provide was a compass course reading, which was worthless since that did not tell the crew whether they were flying toward or away from their destination. Without a bearing, the pilot was unsure in which direction to fly.

There was no question about it now—they were lost. De Angelis offered one possible explanation: his octant had been aboard the plane during the aborted takeoff in Hawaii, and it might have been jarred enough to skew his observations. Even a few degrees could have caused them to fly many miles to the right or left of their destination. The crew asked Canton to fire off anti-aircraft shells, set to explode above the clouds at 7,000 feet, and also to send out search planes in every direction. Nothing worked. Their only hope was to spot a ship, which also proved fruitless.

At 1:30 p.m., the pilot informed Rickenbacker that they had only one hour of fuel remaining. Rickenbacker wrote out a note and gave it to the radio operator to send. It was the last message anyone received from the B-17. Reynolds continued sending out SOS signals while Cherry climbed to 5,000 feet for a better view and shut down two engines to conserve fuel. As the gas gauge neared zero, Cherry began preparing to ditch. Meanwhile, all hands were busy discarding everything not considered essential to survival, including mail, a toolbox, cots, blankets, luggage, and Rickenbacker's briefcase which contained classified material.

Mattresses were propped against the bulkhead to cushion the men from the expected jolt, and everyone donned Mae West life jackets. Three self-inflating rubber rafts were available, two with a listed capacity of five men that Bartek was set to expel by pulling cockpit levers, and a two-man raft rolled up in the radio compartment. Cherry advised that, since the plane weighed twenty-five tons, they should not expect to have more than 30 to 60 seconds to exit the craft after splashdown. Rickenbacker stuffed a map, official papers, and passport into his coat pockets. He also grabbed handkerchiefs and a 60-foot line; both later proved a godsend.

The men braced themselves for the crash as Cherry glided downward. Bartek stood behind the pilot, holding the levers to release the two big rafts. Rickenbacker was strapped to his seat on the right-hand side, having a pillow to protect his face. Adamson was sitting on the deck, bracing his back against a mattress. Reynolds remained at his radio, sending a constant series of SOS signals—hoping that someone somewhere might establish a fix on them. About the time someone yelled, "Only 50 feet left!"

One engine sputtered and died. Rickenbacker glanced out a window and saw that the ocean was rough, with high swells. In a moment, the big plane made a soft but loud bellyflop in the middle of a trough and skipped another 50 feet before stopping against the waning slope of a swell. As crash landings at sea go, this one was about as good as they got. Had Cherry misjudged the waves by only seconds, the plane and its passengers might have sunk immediately.

Green water immediately began gushing through smashed windows, making it impossible to salvage much of the survival equipment. Reynolds suffered from cuts on his hands and face, and his head had struck the radio panel, resulting in more bleeding. Adamson sustained a severely sprained back, but most of the injuries were manageable.

The two five-man rafts and one two-man raft were released by the lever in the cockpit and self-inflated. The pilots exited through the forward hatch and lent a hand to the passengers. Rickenbacker escaped through the above wing hatch. Once outside, he helped the others climb out. The swells were well over six feet high, making the rafts extremely difficult to manage.

Bartek, Adamson, and Rickenbacker were in one five-man raft, and Cherry, Whittaker, and Reynolds were in the other. The small raft was upside down. Righting the raft in the six-foot swells, Kaczmarczyk and De Angelis experienced difficulty getting aboard, but they finally succeeded and were exhausted. Rickenbacker's 60 feet of line had more to do with their salvation than anything else.

The crew members tied the rafts 20 feet apart, allowing them closer contact when problems arose and the camaraderie so important in dire situations. Had the three rafts been allowed to float aimlessly around in the Pacific, it is doubtful that any men would have survived. In all the confusion and yelling between the rafts, the men began looking for the water thermoses that had been so carefully stacked together before the crash. They were gone. They then discovered that the only food they had managed to salvage was four oranges Cherry had stuffed into his jacket pocket. Those water-filled thermos bottles, emergency rations, and the other items stored by an escape hatch would not be seen again.

The men began to take stock of their clothing. Rickenbacker and Adamson were the only two fully dressed. Adamson had his cap and uniform, and Rickenbacker was in a business suit with shirt, tie, and felt hat. Most of the others had shed everything, including their shoes, expecting to have to swim after the crash. The pilots had held onto their leather jackets, but Bartek was wearing only a one-piece jumper.

A quick inventory of possessions showed they had a first-aid kit, a Very pistol with eighteen flares, two hand pumps for bailing water and pumping air into the rafts, two sheath knives, a pair of pliers, a small compass, two collapsible bailing buckets, some patching gear for each raft, pencils, and Rickenbacker's map. Reynolds had grabbed two fishing lines, but there was no bait. The pilots had also kept their pistols.

The men were exhausted, and a few became violently seasick. Adamson's back injury was excruciating, while the others suffered from a variety of cuts and bruises. Sergeant Kaczmarczyk, who had been out of the hospital only a couple of weeks, was in serious trouble. He had swallowed a good deal of seawater and needed more help than the others could provide. As the sun set, the temperature plunged. Although beautiful, a three-quarters moon signalled the start of many long, scorching hot days and cold, lonely nights. And so began the 21-day odyssey, defining once again Eddie's determination to cheat the Reaper.

Eddie was responsible for dividing the oranges, making them last six days, providing some, but very little sustenance. On the eighth day, a bit of luck came their way when a seagull landed on Eddie's head. The men stared wide-eyed in disbelief. "I felt it land upon my head. Slowly, I raised my hand not to frighten it, grabbed it, and wrung its neck."

The men feasted on the raw flesh and bone. The intestines were used as bait, carefully husbanded for the fishing lines, and hooks stored in the life rafts. They got much-needed water from a storm. Sgt. Alexander Kaczmarczyk would later become so desperate for water that he would clandestinely drink seawater. His condition would worsen, and on the 13th day, he would die and be buried at sea.

Cursing one man who prayed for death and dragging back another who tried to drown himself to make more room for the others, Eddie, the grim, indomitable figure, taunted his comrades to stay alive. Hating him every minute, six of these seven survived to be rescued by a patrolling plane that would later find them almost by chance. With their clothing slowly rotting in the seawater and sun, the intense heat of the sun was exacerbated by the constant sloshing of seawater into the rafts, causing blisters to form. Sharks were a continuous reminder of their peril should they enter the water, as they continually thumped the bottom of the rafts. Despite the ominous reminder, all but Eddie and the badly injured Adamson would slide into the water to cool the burning blisters from the intense sun exposure. The sharks would circle but never thankfully attack.

During the third week, they found themselves adrift in a calming sea. Mariners have referred to them as the "Doldrums" for years, entombed in this phenomenon that had instilled terror in the hearts of sailors through many centuries. (Known as the Inter-Tropical Convergence Zone, it no longer threatens powered vessels.) This phenomenon produced severe depression among the raft survivors. Rickenbacker, recognizing this depression, refused to allow it to take hold, harassing, cursing, embarrassing, and casting aspersions on their manhood, all to keep hope alive.

"I think the cussing Rick gave the gang that evening was the masterpiece of his career," said Lt. Whitaker. "In about a minute, he had everyone roaring mad, then he got under their skin individually, finishing up with a broadside at the whole bunch. It was the most wonderful handling of profane language I have ever heard."

All the survivors later believed they owed their lives to Mr. Rickenbacker's iron will. The *Rime of the Ancient Mariner* came to Lt. Whitaker's mind during this period.

Day after day, day after day, we were stuck, not breath or motion.

"As idle as a painted ship, Upon a painted ocean."

On the seventeenth day, their spirits rose as they spotted an aircraft about five miles distant. Some of their signal flares had previously been used in the early days, adrift, as they attempted to be noticed; the others were ruined with the constant exposure to seawater dousing. Shakily standing while hopefully waving, they were not seen. Seeing a raft in the rough sea is like trying to find a flyspeck in a pepper shaker. On the twentieth day, the majority agreed their chances of being rescued would improve if they split up. Captain Cherry set himself adrift from the others in that hope. Rickenbacker was dubious. He would be proven wrong as Captain Cherry's raft was sighted on the second day. The search and rescue for the survivors was about to be shut down that day.

It continued with new vigor when, on the twenty-fourth day, there was news of Cherry's sighting by a single-engine Kingfisher seaplane flying overhead, Captain Cherry's raft. Upon hearing of this sighting, General 'Hap' Arnold immediately rescinded the order to abandon the search, reintroducing a maximum effort to find the downed aviators.

Rickenbacker, Bartek, and Adamson were in one drifting raft, while De Angelis, Whitaker, and Reynolds were in another. Drifting for many days, De Angelis spotted the Island of Nukufetau. Rowing against a reverse surf, they reached the Island completely exhausted. Island natives came to their aid, restoring their hopes of eventual Navy rescue. Meanwhile, unaware of Captain Cherry's rescue, Eddie soon hears the unmistakable sound of another aircraft. Rickenbacker and the other survivors even waved their underwear to be seen. They had been spotted.

The pilot, Lt. William Eadie, landed his Kingfisher aircraft and drifted alongside the raft. He and his radioman 2/c Lester Boutte placed the seriously injured Adamson in the cabin. Lacking room inside, Eddie and Bartek were lifted onto the wings, with Eddie on the left wing, legs dangling; they were secured in sitting positions with Boutte straddling the rear cockpit, held onto Rickenbacker and Bartek by what was left of their collars.

Lt. Eadie, now unable to fly, taxied the aircraft forty-five miles until it rendezvoused with a PT Boat Tender, USS Hilo (PG-58). There, they were transferred and rushed to a hospital on the Island of Funafuti.

The atheist Whittaker and the agnostic Adamson were converted to a faith they had never known before when they witnessed what they called a miracle. A rainstorm had been seen approaching their rafts when it was suddenly turned away for no apparent reason. Private John Bartek, who had held on to and read frequently from his small bible, began reading and pleading for Jesus to turn the storm back their way. During this plea, as the men watched, the storm bent back in their direction, eventually dumping several inches of much-needed and welcome water upon the men. Clutching the medal given to him earlier by Ms. Russell, which was still in his pocket, Adamson gave thanks.

Whittaker was later heard saying, "There are no atheists in foxholes or in drifting rafts."

Upon hearing they had been given up for lost, he said, "Everyone knows that Eddie Rickenbacker always comes back, and I figured my wife thought the same about me."

Capt. Eddie, as he preferred to be called, would later continue his trip to Brisbane and meet with General Douglas MacArthur. Upon returning to the United States, Captain Eddie was greeted with ticker-tape parades, parties, and accolades from a grateful nation.

The Grim Reaper would catch up to Capt. Eddie, when he cashed in his ninth life on July 24, 1973, at the age of 82.

RIP Capt. Eddie!

Chapter Thirty~Nine
"CHANCE~VOUGHT F8 CRUSADER"

USS Shangri-La Cva 38 1970 Vietnam

The Last of the Gunfighters!

Navy CDR (Ret.) Doug Simpson was an RF-8G Photo Reconnaissance Crusader pilot who flew off of the USS Ticonderoga, CVA 14, and the USS Shangri-La, CVA 38 aircraft carrier (among others) from 1968 to 1970, his last year in the Vietnam conflict.

I had the good fortune to meet and fly with Doug many years later, when he was the chief pilot of a corporate flight department based in Tampa, FL. I was a "new hire" captain, engaged to fly the Falcon 900EX aircraft in his charge. Our friendship and memories have endured through the years.

The history of the F-8 aircraft began in the mid to late 1950s when the Chance-Vought F-8 Crusader replaced the F-7 aircraft.

It became the first operationally equipped jet aircraft to fly faster than 1,000 mph.

On 16 July 1957, future astronaut Major John H. Glenn, Jr. flew an F-8 aircraft in a record transcontinental flight, taking off from Los Alamitos, CA, and reaching Floyd Bennett Field, New York, in 3 hours, 22 minutes, and 50.05 seconds. Vought's F-8 Crusader successfully bridged the gap between the days of close-quarters dogfighting and the supersonic era of long-range missile engagements. It was once said: "If you are out of F-8s, you're out of fighters." It was "The Last of the Gunfighters" with armaments of four 20 mm Mk 12 cannons with 144 rounds per gun and up to four AIM-9 Sidewinder AAMs or eight 113 kg (250 lb.) Mk 81 or 227 kg (500 lb) Mk 82 bombs; or eight Zuni rockets; or two AGM-12A or 12B Bullpup attack missiles.

Crusaders flew their first combat missions, triggering cameras instead of weapons during photo-reconnaissance flights over Cuba during the Cuban Missile Crisis in October 1962. The 2000 movie *Thirteen Days* dramatizes that crisis inside the Kennedy White House and accurately depicts one of these high-threat, high-speed, low-level RF-8 missions.

Some of Cdr. Doug's adrenaline-pumping F-8 reminisces were recounted to me while he and I crewed the Falcon 900 on more than a few adventurous trips together. A feature of flying any supersonic jet will no doubt pique the memories of pilots who piloted such aircraft. A few of his recollections, locked away in his memory banks over time, were recounted to me during those airborne hours. Some are recounted below.

"One of the scariest things that ever happened to me in the F-8 was during a cross-country flight from the East Coast to the West. It was the middle of December 1981, and I was returning to San Diego, CA (Miramar), from Washington, DC (Andrews

233

AFB), on the second half of a 'Round Robin' flight, with a stop in OKC (Oklahoma City) for fuel. I had been based at Andrews while in the Reserves and still had a locker where I kept an Air Force winter flight suit. I had never worn one before, but for some reason, I put on that winter flight suit for the return flight. It proved fortuitous."

"It was a night flight, flying at FL 410 and .92 Mach, flying over Tennessee. The F-8 had a three-panel bulletproof windscreen. All was well as I settled in for a routine flight. Suddenly, the left front windscreen blew out of the cockpit canopy! My gloves, which had been resting on the instrument panel, and all my maps just disappeared. There I was in a 700-knot wind and FL410. The noise was tremendous! Now freezing my butt off, I immediately reduced power to idle, speed brakes out, and descended as rapidly as possible. I needed to shout at the Center above the noise that I was in a rapid emergency descent and to clear all airspace below me. I leveled the descent at FL 100 (Ten thousand ft.) and reduced speed to 200 Kts. (The only speed at which I could hear someone on the radio).

"Asking for the nearest airport, I was vectored towards the nearest suitable airport, SDF (Louisville, KY). I yelled that I would speed up until about 20 miles from SDF and asked for a frequency on which I could call them back. I would not be able to hear until I again slowed. When I was about 20 miles and slowing, I advised that I was back on frequency and could once again hear transmissions. I was informed that the airport was at 12 o'clock and 18 miles distant.

"Do you have it in sight?" asked ATC.

"No, but I see a lot of flashing red lights. That must be it."

"Roger, they are for you. You are cleared to land."

"They never determined why or how that event could have happened. Everything had blown away from the aircraft. They had no evidence indicating why this occurred, but it had cracked the entire frame around the cockpit. Unbelievably, the repair took only three days and was completed by a Navy Senior Chief and an E3 Striker. (Navy Vets will recognize that rank). I was soon returning to San Diego's Miramar Field."

"I also recall while based at Andrews AFB in Washington, I was on a test flight heading out over the Atlantic at 1.4 Mach when a tremendous BANG occurred. It immediately got my attention. A sudden compressor stall just scared the hell out of me. All of my instruments were normal, with no indication of anything amiss. To be safe and about 100+ miles from shore, I returned to Andrews and landed uneventfully. Nothing was ever found amiss with the engine, but it got my attention. Strange! And yet another time, I participated in carrier qualifications on the Nimitz. There had never been any F-8 aircraft operational aboard the Nimitz." A test pilot did a study for the Nimitz regarding F-8 operations to be conducted aboard. He determined that the maximum wind could not be more than 35 kts across the bow to land an F-8. On this day, the wind was 50 kts. The exercise was initially canceled until the Air Boss devised a plan. They decided to back down the ship in reverse at 15 knots to mitigate the wind to 35 kts. The ship was going in reverse at 15 knots. (Yankee ingenuity)

"When landing on a carrier, you come off the 180 and cross the wake to set up the landing. However, in this instance, the wake was off the bow, not the stern, which made for an exciting exercise to trap successfully. Lining up without the wake was a little bit unusual, requiring an intense degree of focus. One of my scarier recollections was when we were engaged in night quails off of Gitmo (Guantanamo Bay, Cuba). I got a bit low on the final approach to the ship. All approaches were CCA approaches. (Carrier Controlled Approach.) At 3/4 mile, you need to 'call the ball.' It was then that the ball started to go low. It is not good unless immediately corrected, or you will end up low at the ramp. I poured on power to get to the glide slope, then pulled power off, more than I needed as it turned out, and the ball went from green to yellow and back to red, then nothing, no color. I added full power, came up over the ramp, did a high dip (pulled power, pushed nose, added power, pulled nose, all in one second), and caught the #4 wire. The LSO thought that was an OK pass. He gave me an OK pass! I thought he should have waved me off well before the ramp. 'No, no,' he said. 'That was OK.'

I said, 'Let's look at it on the Plat.' (It had a small screen where recent carrier landings could be viewed.)

We both watched the video. It displayed all aircraft lights, including Port and Starboard, Lights, as well as taillight Then, all lights disappeared momentarily below the fantail, reappearing instantly high over the ramp. Upon reviewing the video, he then agreed it wasn't that good. That is an understatement of a horrible approach. I thought, you dumb shit, you damn near killed yourself!

The SHANGRI-LA returned to the western Pacific in 1970 after a ten-year absence. She got underway from Mayport, FL, on March 5, stopped at Rio de Janeiro, Brazil, from March 13 to the 16, and headed east through the Atlantic and Indian Oceans. It was during this deployment that Doug remembered yet another remarkable event.

"We were 2200 miles from the nearest bingo field. (Emergency refueling) It was decided to exercise the air wing. We were told, 'Don't fly too far away. Just come back in for a landing. As I walked out to the deck, I discovered it was pitching

16 to 25 ft. as mountainous waves battered the ship. This was Stupid, especially since you had to land at the carrier. I tried to find something wrong with the aircraft so I wouldn't have to fly. Unfortunately, I couldn't find anything wrong with it and had to go. I was following the CAG on take-off and landing. On his landing, he hit the deck pretty hard, bending the tail hook and damaging the aircraft, but he did catch a wire. You must understand that the deck is either falling away from you or coming up to meet you with vengeance. It took me six wave-offs to get back on board. I made it by doing what we called 'Deck Spotting' rather than the ball. After I got aboard, I was second to last aboard. The exercise was canceled as the carrier plowed through the gale-wracked Atlantic. As we continued, we encountered three typhoons with titanic-sized waves broaching the bow 20 ft. above the 80 ft. deck. Two aircraft were scrapped because of saltwater damage."

The 'Shang' arrived in Subic Bay, RP, on April 04 and launched combat sorties from Yankee station during the next seven months. Her tours of duty at Yankee Station were punctuated by frequent logistics trips to Subic Bay, visits to Manila, RP, and Hong Kong, BCC, in October, and 12 days in dry-dock at Yokosuka, Japan, in July.

Doug tells another story of a Recon flight over North Vietnam.

"While on a Recon flight over N. Vietnam generally required about 16 other aircraft to assist. On one such sortie, my projected route was from Vinh in the North to Mu Gia (Moo Geea) pass." A Sam Site was reported north of Vinh, and I was asked to get a picture. A Sam site picked me up as I approached Vinh and started my run. I looked down and saw what appeared to be a large explosion. I thought it could have been a missile exploding on the rack. I immediately got a light on the panel showing I had a big lock on, a LOW PRF aural warning, followed by a Double Time HIGH PRF indicating a launch.

"I 'broke down' (descended), turning left to indicate where a missile might be coming from and banked into it, putting on G's, pulling into the missile to see if it was tracking me. The answer was to do a barrel roll or something much different than expected because a missile with its tiny wings could not follow an abrupt movement. You have to play Chicken with it. I went down the VIN River at 50 feet and 700 knots. My F8 wingman, who was loaded out with guns and missiles, lost me for a while. We eventually returned together, completed the photo run, and returned to the ship. This was September of 1970 and my last mission."

Doug made about 300 traps, which he feels are not that many. Many guys have over 1,000 traps. He was on active duty for 16 years and then served an additional seven more years in the reserves. He began flying the F-8 in 1967, accumulating 2,800 hours of flight time in the reconnaissance version (RF-8G). This is a very high number of hours, but it's not the most F-8 flight hours. That honor was held by Doug's former commanding officer, Admiral Bud Flagg, who had 3,300 hours in the F-8. Admiral Flag (Ret.) and his wife had the misfortune of being passengers aboard American Airlines Flight #77 on the fateful day it was hijacked and later crashed into the Pentagon. The aircraft struck one floor below the Admiral's old office. Knowing the man, Doug remains convinced Admiral Flagg would not have allowed that. "He most probably would have been killed during his attempt to stop the hijackers."

A more personal memory of Doug's was when we were on an extended trip in the Falcon 900; we relished a welcome rest overnight (RON) in LAX after a very long day of flying. We had dinner and drinks at a bar in Marina Del Rey later that evening, and we both had too much to drink. I became pretty hammered. Doug had fewer drinks than I because the next day, he told me he had carried me over his shoulder, fireman style, from the bar after he had called a taxi, which drove us back to the Marriott where we were staying, depositing me on the bed.

When I awoke the following day, I had been stripped of all my clothes and was lying on the floor with my clothes strewn about the room. When I called him to ask what the hell happened and why I was naked when I awoke, he said: "All I did was drop you on the bed. You must have stripped yourself."

I had no memory of any of that. "You had been as drunk as I was," I said.

He replied: "Yeah, but I didn't tell anybody. You told everybody, so it was time to get you out of there."

Much later that day, as we were getting off the elevator and proceeding to check out, a fellow approached, claiming to have witnessed me across Doug's shoulder the previous night as I was being transported on his shoulder to my room. I was embarrassed!

Thank God I was with Doug that night. He is 6'4" and weighs about 240 lbs. I will never know how he fits in the cockpit of that F-8.

The F8 was a Mach 1.8 aircraft, but it seldom reached that speed. The plane had what Doug called an "Image Motion Compensator," which allowed the film to cross the camera's face to take clear pictures regardless of speed. It was a fantastic device!

Doug had flown 150 photo missions over North Vietnam. His Navy career exemplifies honor, courage, patriotism, and pride in the dedication to freedom illustrated in the promises of our founding Republic.

Well done!

Thank you, Commander!

*F-8J Crusaders of VF-191 "Satan Kittens" Prepare to launch from the USS Oriskany (CV-34) *1970**

Bibliography

(Chapter Thirty-One) Source: Wikipedia

References:

- "What Happened on July 23, 1983?" OnThisDay.com. Retrieved December 24, 2022.
- "Fuel-starved engines blamed for crash landing of Ottawa." Ottawa Citizen. Staff and news services. July 25, 1983. p. 1.
- "Jetliner glides down on race track." Calgary Herald. Canadian Press. July 25, 1983. p. A1.

(Chapter Thirty-Two) Source: Wikipedia

References:

- Crossette, Barbara (September 10, 2001). "Jet Pilot Who Saved 304 Finds Heroism Tainted." The New York Times. ISSN 0362-4331. Retrieved August 21, 2007.
- "How a civilian aircraft in distress set a world glider record." We Are The Mighty. August 14, 2020. Retrieved May 25, 2021. "Air Transat Flight 236: The Azores Glider" (PDF). Retrieved July 27, 2010

(Chapter Thirty-Four) Source: Wikipedia

References:

- Allison Wright, Nancy. "On Wings of Faith: Navigating the First Day/Night Transcontinental." Airmail Pioneers. Retrieved February 28, 2021.
- Pope, Nancy A. "Jack Knight Saves the Airmail." Smithsonian National Postal Museum. Retrieved March 1, 2021.

(Chapter Thirty-Five) Source: Wikipedia

References:

- Udet, Ernst (1981). Stanley M. Ulanoff (ed.). Ace of the Iron Cross. Arco.
- Udet, Ernst (1935). Mein Fliegerleben (My Life of Flying). Berlin, Germany: Im Deutschen Verlag, Ullstein A.G.
- Van Ishoven, Armand (1979). The Fall of an Eagle: The Life of Fighter Ace Ernst Udet. Kimb

(Chapters Thirty-Six / Thirty-Seven / Thirty-Eight) Source: Wikipedia:

References:

- Rickenbacker, Edward V. Rickenbacker: an Autobiography. Englewood Cliffs: Prentice- Hall, Inc., 1967.
- Lewis, W. David. Eddie Rickenbacker: An American Hero in the Twentieth Century, Johns Hopkins University Press, Baltimore.
- Courage, John F. Ross, Lost at Sea, John Wukovits, Ace of Aces, Jeffers H. Paul

ABOUT THE AUTHOR

From the author's early years as a 'freight dog' pilot flying old WWII aircraft, he was mentored by many former WWII pilots who had experienced hundreds of terrifying airborne hours over mountainous terrain. Mountains that exceeded the heights the aircraft could never attain in conditions of limited control due to often 'tornadic' winds aloft, zero forward visibility, and icing conditions, all due to extreme weather conditions while flying 'The Hump' (Himalayas).

The mentoring and lessons absorbed from these men, accompanied by much frustration, were not always pleasant, but always well-intended. Lessons hard learned are often forever remembered and were sometimes called upon to save the day. Applying many of those long-ago lessons has stood the test of time for the author, translating quickly and efficiently to many of today's complex aircraft he has since flown.

Those experiences were put to good use during a long and rewarding career, proving beneficial to many even as the 'torch was passed' during the author's many years instructing and certifying professional pilots as an FAA-designated check airman in several different types of private jet aircraft, and pilots from around the world.

Now retired, he lives in South Carolina with his wife of forty years, his Sheep-a-Doodle, Quinn, and a hilarious kitty named Dolly. The author occasionally takes to the air, flying with friends on weekends for fun and pleasure.